Aurea Vidyā Collection*

——— 23 ———

* For a complete list of titles see Publications on page 131.

This book was originally published in Italian in 1979 as
Raphael, *Essenza e scopo dello yoga*, Le Vie iniziatiche
al Trascendente, by Associazione Ecoculturale Parmenides
(formerly Edizioni Āśram Vidyā), Rome

ISBN 978-1-931406-36-9

On the cover: 'The calling of Peter and Andrew'. Detail from the 'Maestà' of Duccio di Buoninsegna. Museo dell'Opera della Metropolitana, Siena

RAPHAEL
(Āśram Vidyā Order)

ESSENCE AND PURPOSE OF YOGA

Initiatory ways to the Transcendent

AUREA VIDYĀ

'Various are the ways by which the goal of spiritual achievement can be attained: the love of the Beautiful which intoxicates the poet; that devotion for the One and that cognitive ascent which constitute the aspiration of the philosopher; that love and those prayers with which devoted, ardent spirits yearn, in moral purity, for perfection. There are the great Master-Ways which lead to that zenith – beyond the worldly, the current, and the particular – where we can rise to the immediate presence of the Infinite which streams, with its effulgence, from the depths of the soul.'[1]

[1] Words attributed to Plotinus.

CONTENTS

INTRODUCTION

Man goes in search of the Unknown because his present position of consciousness is incomplete and in conflict. In moments of great tension, he wonders, 'When shall I be able to find peace and serenity, the joy and beauty of accord? When shall I be able to be happy?'

It is clear that such questions imply that the individual has not found happiness, or peace, or harmony. And this 'unfulfilled consciousness' is bound to lead irresistibly to the search for complete fullness, such that all individual problems can eventually be solved.

If we acknowledge that the being is in conflict, fragmentary, and incomplete, two questions arise:

1. What is the nature of that serenity which can provide fulfilment?
2. What is the nature of the practical means for realising that serenity?

There is no doubt that the individual has always directed his steps towards attaining happiness and existential freedom. Happiness constitutes a psychological aspect of enjoyment; it is an effect, and so it presupposes an action, a movement, a relationship with things/events[1] which can actually produce the state of happiness.

If we observe the *action* man has undertaken in the course of time, we can see that it has been aimed at acquiring things that are material/sensory. We would say that his action has always been centripetal and such as can satisfy the senses and therefore the 'sensory ego'. Man has believed that by acquiring he will find well-being and solve his problem of incompleteness. So happiness has become synonymous with the enjoyment of 'something': sex; power of any order or degree; things; and so on. But, as we have seen, this happiness belongs to the realm of the egoic sense. In fact, the enjoyment of the senses is governed, of its nature, by an ebb and flow that is not *constant*, with the result that the ego/being finds itself unhappy even in the very act of possessing. Consequently, however rich we are, we may still be unhappy; whatever power is in our hands, we may still be unhappy; and however loved we are, we may still be unhappy and unfulfilled.

All of this leads us to understand that this kind of sensory/dualistic/egoic happiness does not give true fulfilment or grant that deep peace which creates harmony. We must also acknowledge that if this happiness is unreal and inconstant, so must be the means/objects which are used as its basis and support. On the other hand, an unreal (relative) cause produces an effect which is equally unreal. We can state that all the objects on which sensory happiness or unhappiness depends are – in the final analysis – bringers of unhappiness. It is only

[1] The purpose of the forward slash [/] in this text is to show the relationship of the two or more items either side of it. Thus it may indicate a single concept seen from two different perspectives or a concept of unity or wholeness. However, it is left to the intuition of the reader to appreciate the specific nuance imparted by the use of the slash each time it occurs.

our ignorance (*avidyā*) that actually makes us experience pleasure in experiences that *potentially* constitute a source of conflict. A world of relativities contains, deep down, the seed of impermanence and unhappiness. Closer reflection allows us to acknowledge that attaching our consciousness to these means/objects leads us to suffering. Then what is that happiness which can make us fulfilled? What is that happiness which does not deceive us and divert us from the true, authentic *pax profunda*, which is ever identical to itself?

We have seen that every means/object related to acquisition and the senses is unable to lead to ultimate happiness, or bliss, because it itself is an instrument that is contingent and changeable. How can something that is relative and incomplete grant that which is unvarying and complete? How can there be a constant in the world of becoming?

How can there be stillness in movement? Or stability in ebb and flow?

If we desire bliss, it is obvious that we shall have to direct our steps towards the realm of the Constant, the Unchanging, and the eternally valid. This Constant exists, for others have *experienced* and *expressed* it.[1]

Only by following this road can we be certain of finding fulfilment and the *pax profunda*: that peace which is desired, hoped, and yearned for by all human beings.

Now, to what do the Constant, the eternally valid, and the Unchanging correspond? Science itself provides us with the answer: the Absolute, because whatever is relative presupposes something absolute and has meaning only when compared to what is absolute. Even Einstein's theory of relativity is based on something absolute, that

---

[1] See *Vivekacūḍāmaṇi*, 'The Realised Man', verse 536 *et seqq.* Translation from the Sanskrit and commentary by Raphael. Aurea Vidyā, New York.

is, on the measurable nature of the space-time continuum. The constant is that which is ever identical to itself, that which depends on nothing but itself, that which undergoes no change or mutation; in other words, that which has an *absolute* value.

The task, therefore, of someone who desires Happiness with a capital 'H' is to *discriminate*, *discern*, and find – within the unceasing flow of the things around him – the Absolute, the Unchanging, that Happiness which never deceives or disappears but bestows peace, order, harmony, proper relationships in society and throughout the world. We have to acknowledge that social disharmony is a result of the individual's disharmony, and if we wish to resolve the question of just social accord, the very first need is for harmony and just accord to be experienced and to operate in the consciousness of the individual. Strife and warfare, hatred and every kind of deficiency are objectivised reflections of the individual's struggle with himself and his alienation from the principial, absolute realm, the realm of Constant.

If we have appreciated that only the constant, absolute dimension can resolve the agonising problems of existence, then we have to consider what are the practical means, among so many options, and what is the most suitable road, to take us to completeness. The means – we repeat – must be such as will take us to the 'constant', because if they lead to the individualised, conflictual ego, they cannot reveal the state of 'what one is'. If we accept this thesis, we shall have to eliminate from the field of our possibilities many means that are normally considered valid. All that culture and literature, as well as that science which operates exclusively in the individualised world of the senses, must be demythologised, because, at its root, it does not resolve the real, pressing problem of the being; on the contrary, it magnifies it and multiplies the difficulties. As we have seen, the means must be such as will touch what we would call the transcendent aspect of the empirical ego: means that will act as a bridge and will be able, through their intrinsic mode of operation, to be a ferry to the higher bank of being. Such means belong to a realm that is called 'sacred' in relation to the individualised realm known as 'profane'. There is no opposition between the two realms; being polar, they resolve into the *point/principle*. There are two roads: that of *avidyā* (metaphysical ignorance, profane perspective) and that of *vidyā* (Knowledge, sacred perspective).[1]

> 'Two [things], in truth, are within the indestructible, within That which transcends *Brahmā*, within the infinite: there, deeply hidden, lie knowledge and ignorance. Ignorance, in truth, is destructible, while knowledge, in truth, is everlasting. But He who regulates knowledge and ignorance is other [than these].'[1]

To be precise, *avidyā* operates in the world of the relative and phenomenal, the world of movement, mirage, and the empirical ego. *Vidyā* is concerned with the realm of Principle, the Real/Absolute, the Constant, the eternally valid.

Vidyā is the traditional Science of the earliest times, with its various ramifications in the East and the West. It encompasses two phases of teaching: *apara*, knowledge that is lower or not supreme; and *para*, higher or supreme Knowledge. To the first phase (*apara*) belong those teachings which lead to the universal Seed, to *Īśvara*, to *saguṇa Brahman*, to the God-Person (with attributes) who pervades everything, and to the single,

---

[1] *Śvetāśvatara Upaniṣad*, 1,5,1.

all-pervading ‘substance’. To the second phase (*para*) belongs the pure metaphysical Teaching which leads to the unconditioned Absolute without attributes, to the metaphysical Zero, to *nirguṇa Brahman*, to the One without a second.

THE PERSONAL AND IMPERSONAL ASPECTS OF THE DIVINE

The spiritual Tradition has always posited a conception of the Divine with attributes or qualifications of form (*saguṇa*) and a conception without form, stripped of all specific and personal attributes (*nirguṇa*). *Nirguṇa* and *saguṇa* are therefore not two convenient formulas of this or that philosophical or theological school, but the conception of Reality in itself, at two levels.

The *saguṇa* reality corresponds to 'Our Father which art in heaven', the one who gives us life as the creator; the dispenser of grace; the one we invoke, love, and frequently fear; the creator, preserver, and transformer of all life's forms and compounds; the law-giver; the one who comprises all of the highest 'qualities' conceivable by man. In Him we live and move and have our being.

'Be ye perfect, even as your Father which is in heaven is perfect'[1]: these words of Jesus constitute the highest aspiration for those who conceive of God as a person. When we say that God represents the single reality, we mean that He is the single seed from which sprout the

---

[1] St Matthew, 5:48.

indefinite[1] universal conditions of forms. There is nothing in the universe that is not contained within the seed/principle. There is no act, occurrence, or effect that is not already, like power and cause, within the divine seed. Every possible empirical truth is nothing but a fragment of the one Truth. All worlds and all beings are 'projections' of the primary cause, and to it they return. This is a teaching which relates everything to the Unity of life, to the homogeneity of the original substance. In philosophical terms, it corresponds to the ontological level.

Empirical science has discovered that matter cannot be considered to consist of so many particles, each different from the other (the pluralistic conception), but should be thought of as a homogeneous, electronic mass, as energy, and hence as light. We may say that science has discovered the unity of matter, whereas the *yogi*/philosopher has discovered the unity of life at all three levels: gross/material (the field of science), subtle, and causal.

The *nirguṇa* reality corresponds to the Principle, which is without form, attributes, qualifications, or names. It is the root or foundation of all that exists. The God-Person is none other than a reflection of the *nirguṇa*. The *nirguṇa* reality stands for the unparalleled Absolute, the unqualified, the permanent, the unchanging, and the constant. If the *saguṇa* reality is the manifest (gross, subtle, and causal), the *nirguṇa* reality is the Unmanifest, that which is beyond the realm of 'nature'.

---

[1] See *Tat tvam asi*, page 54, 'We need to look carefully at these two terms: "infinite" and "indefinite". "Infinite", in its purest meaning, is "beyond all limit, series, beginning, and end; beyond all conditioning, number, point, line, and constraint". The "indefinite" is a *series* of data which, although they may extend indefinitely, are nevertheless finite and under the law of necessity. Thus a series of numbers, which can be combined indefinitely with each other, is still *finite*.' Aurea Vidyā, New York.

If the *saguṇa* reality is Being which *appears* as many, the *nirguṇa* reality is Non-Being. Because it has no attributes, this reality may be conceived in terms of negation, in the sense that, within it, are negated all those names or determinations which are, on the other hand, peculiar to the *saguṇa* reality. Negation, therefore, refers to the fact that *nirguṇa* cannot be expressed. On the other hand, how could we describe something that has no relationships, no qualifications, and no attributes? Moreover, a description is always a truth of relationship and is therefore relative (relative to something else). If the *saguṇa* represents the initial and principial movement, the *nirguṇa* represents the Unmoved, the true 'unmoved Mover' which supports everything.

Someone might think that there are two realities. There are not two realities (moreover there would then be duality or absolute multiplicity, which would be absurd); there is a *single reality*, which is seen by beings who are caught up in the process of becoming now as *saguṇa*, now as *nirguṇa*. It is ever the One, considered from different perspectives, according to the different levels of receiving it. In the same way – to give an example – matter can be considered from different points of view as mass (solid) or as energy (without form); but mass and energy are expressions of a single reality.

BLISS AND THE PATHWAYS OF ATTAINING IT

We spoke earlier of the means, the pathways, or roads which lead to the *saguṇa* or ontological perspective and to the *nirguṇa* or supreme reality. Now we shall proceed to a deeper investigation of the practical ways.

According to traditional philosophy, the human being is composed of three elements which represent a unity: body, soul, and Spirit.

The Spirit is the spark that is linked to the Principle. The soul is the *logos*, the plastic intermediary. The body/individuality is the individualised egoic compound whose vehicle of expression is discursive thought.

The movement of the soul has two aspects: it can look to the empirical and phenomenal world, the world which is apparent and transitory; and it can look to the world of Spirit. Thus it can expend its energy on the plane of objectivity and differentiation, or it can recollect itself within itself, return to its deepest essence, and there attain the Spirit, which is indescribable bliss (*ānanda*). The return to Unity is the work of freedom and liberation from the empirical world of form and phenomenon.

Individuality is a reflection of the soul, and the soul is a reflection of the Spirit. As the reflection of soul-consciousness 'descends', it becomes identified with the various individualised bodies and with the qualities they express, thus modifying the universal qualities: for example, through egoic individuality, love becomes the sensory desire to appropriate or self-love; the spiritual, universal will of being turns into self-affirmation, sef-assertiveness; and noumenal, synthetic knowledge turns into thought that is discursive, empirical, selective, differentiated and concerning quantity.[1]

Individuality is therefore expressed through will, feeling, and knowing: these are the three supports by which one can begin to make contact with the soul and then with the Spirit.

Rājayoga, *Bhaktiyoga*, and *Jñānayoga* base their *sādhanā* on these three elements: *Rāja* on will, *Bhakti* on feeling, *Jñāna* on knowing.

Although each individual can manifest itself through all three aspects or less, it has a single dominant note, with the result that some are polarised on the plane of knowing, some on the plane of feeling, and some on the plane of will.

In addition to these three fundamental types of *yoga*, there are also *Mantrayoga*, for those who are susceptible to sound (although sound is made use of in almost all types of *yoga*); *Haṭhayoga*, for those who are polarised within the physical/living body; *Tantrayoga*, for those who are susceptible to the universal dynamic energy (*śakti*); and others.

It is good to clarify that every type of *yoga* has, as its goal, union with the Principle, the liberation of the soul from the constrictions of phenomenal individuality, and its reintegration into the Spirit; this entails the realisation of the whole, complete being. The being is Spirit and has to re-discover itself as such. *Yoga* is a practical discipline, notwithstanding its high degree of philosophical speculation. It is not a system of techniques

---

[1] To go deeper into these aspects see aphorisms 71-72, Chapter 'The Fire of Life' in *The Threefold Pathway of Fire* by Raphael. Aurea Vidyā, New York.

which reaches a point of exhaustion within the realm of the individual; it is not a psychological system for solving psychical conflicts; it is not simply a method for finding personal peace and quiet or psychosomatic health. But it is a 'raft' which, when wisely used, transports the soul 'from the unreal to the real, from the mortal to the immortal, from darkness to light'.[1]

If man, through an act of free will, has sundered himself from the universal context, thus weakening the connection, thread, or umbilical cord with the father, the divine Principle, the One, and so on (according to the various terminologies), then *yoga* is the instrument that can resolve the 'scissure' or the 'fall'[2]. If *yoga* loses sight of this end, it is not true *yoga*, whether it be *Tantra*, *Rāja*, *Haṭha*, or any other.

It is good to keep insisting that the goal of *yoga*, as such, is to guide the soul that is within us back to the divine Soul, which means that doing mere physical exercises to take care of the body or merely theorising about the philosophy of *yoga* does not mean practising *yoga*. To practise *yoga*, there needs to be a thirst for liberation, a yearning for our divine counterpart – one needs to have that *Eros* (a thirst or yearning for the Intelligible) of which Plato speaks. Without these, it is a mere parody of *yoga*, and sometimes, even worse, a counterfeit.

As long as no specific group arrogates to itself the right to exclusive possession of the teaching and practice in order to reach Being, *yoga* can be accepted and practised even in the cultural and religious context in which one normally finds oneself. *Yoga* is a spiritual

---

[1] See *Bṛhadāraṇyaka Upaniṣad,* 1,3,28.

[2] For this subject, see 'The "Fall" of the Soul' in *The Pathway of Non-Duality* by R. Aurea Vidyā, New York.

Science – if one may expresses it like this – which can be followed by anyone who is free from prejudices and dogmatic fanaticism.

To speak of the various types of *yoga* is a difficult undertaking, because the subject is vast and true *yoga*, being a *living experience*, cannot be described. However, to give an indication, we may refer to some of them.

> 'Various are the ways by which the goal of spiritual achievement can be attained: the love of the Beautiful which intoxicates the poet; that devotion for the One and that cognitive ascent which constitute the aspiration of the philosopher; that love and those prayers with which devoted, ardent spirits yearn, in moral purity, for perfection. There are the great Master-Ways which lead to that zenith – beyond the worldly, the current, and the particular – where we can rise to the immediate presence of the Infinite which streams, with its effulgence, from the depths of the soul.'[1]

It is thought that the *Vedas* contemplate three resolutive moments which relate to action, worship, and knowledge.

The various types of *yoga* develop by focusing on these three ways of approaching the Divine. On the other hand, it needs to be considered that the way of knowledge, the way of will, and the way of feeling (reflection, activity, emotion) cannot be separated from the context of our consciousness; they are moments of a single process and transient aspects of a single reality: the individual.

Let us recall once more that the ultimate essence of *yoga* is the joining and union of the individualised consciousness with the divine consciousness. The human being is a sundered, separated, fragmentary entity; it

[1] These words attributed to Plotinus are drawn from the 'Introduction' of S. Radhakrishnan to the *Bhagavadgītā*, (Italian edition).

expresses only a tiny part of its total string of consciousness. In its nature it is universal and cosmic, but in its illusory egoity it is individual and particular. If we glance at the various types of *yoga*, we may note that they begin from the first step of the ladder – the training of the physical body – and end at the summit when they make contact with the *mens informalis*, or pure reason.

Thus *Haṭhayoga* views the body and the vital functions as instruments of perfection and realisation.

Bhaktiyoga is concerned with the emotional body, making it ever more pliable and full of love for the beloved, so as to effect that 'breaking of levels' which is necessary for Union.

Rājayoga deals with the mind and its various qualifications and movements, and in particular with its volitional aspect. By realising a centre of consciousness which is as steady as a fulcrum, it initiates a process of co-ordination, integration, mastery, transmutation, and transcendence of the imprisoning individualised energies in such a way as to consume with fire all the obstacles that prevent *kaivalya*, the realisation of the *ātman*, or liberation from *avidyā*.

Karmayoga takes action as support for the ascent, and, by leading it into a perfect act of giving, it breaks the centripetal egocentricity of the 'shadow' which is evinced in the world of *saṁsāra* (becoming). Through right and just action, and through abandoning the fruits of action, the individual is transcended.

Jñānayoga works on the intellect in its highest expression, and by means of discrimination (*viveka*) effected through intellectual reflection (*vicara*) it succeeds in separating reality from non-reality. It is a process of selection and synthesis; as absolute values are discerned ever more clearly, the consciousness rises from the particular to the universal, from differentiation to the Undifferentiated.

Asparśayoga (*asparśa* means 'without contact or support') directs its *sādhanā* (discipline) straight to the Absolute, the Unconditioned, and by awakening the absolute nature of Being it urges the consciousness of the disciple to anchor itself directly in the eternal constant, which is unborn and without cause, effect, or change.

The aim is to realise – unhesitatingly, and through an act of truly outstanding courage – a direct flight to that which transcends time, space, and causality and to remain there firmly without 'descending' again to the realm of the sensible. This is the *yoga* of 'lightning': either the consciousness is anchored in Identity or it finds itself once more on the plane of the conceptualised and the deforming world of the phenomenal. It is the 'Way of Fire' which instantly incinerates *māyā* and its effects. It is the *yoga* 'without support', because – unlike the other types of *yoga*, which base their *sādhanā* on emotion, on will, on the discriminating mind, on the physical body, or on other aspects – this *yoga* is not based on inner or outer qualitative factors. Here it is a question of grasping – directly and with an act of total, complete self-transformation – the sense of the Absolute, the metaphysical Zero, the Unqualified (*nirguṇa*), and this implies *rediscovering oneself*, not thinking about oneself.

This *yoga* teaches that 'journeying ... one never arrives'[1]; by desiring, one never ceases to desire; by conceptualising now one thing and now another, the mind never comes to silence; by relying on expressive qualities of *māyā*, one never escapes from *māyā*. One who wishes to stand still must necessarily stop walking.

---

[1] *Samyutta Nikāya* I,62.

Those who wish to break the chains of desire must cease desiring; those who wish for mental silence must refrain from thinking; and those who wish to rise above the bondage of *māyā* must not dabble with its products, however refined they may be.

Asparśayoga makes no concession to ambiguousness and brooks no delay for a consideration, within its dynamic, of the factor of time – and therefore of history and evolution – because the timeless cannot be accessed in time or through time.

Evolution does not lead to the Constant, but always to *saṁsāra*. The Absolute cannot depend on steps or stages of evolution or, therefore, on conditions of time and space. The Absolute *is*, and only those who have the strength, the power, and the heroic will to Be discover themselves as Being. Only those who are bold enough to *find themselves* as Totality discover themselves to be Totality.[1]

---

[1] For a wider explanation see: 'Colourless Fire. Realisation according to Traditional Metaphysics' in *The Threefold Pathway of Fire*, op. cit.

THE ETHICS OF YOGA

Not being a religion (in the generally accepted meaning of this word) or a unilateral creed reserved for Eastern members or groups, *yoga* may be considered, especially in the West, as having no ethics or even a spiritual or initiatory 'vision' or philosophy, or whatever we wish to call it. Nothing could be more mistaken. As a spiritual discipline, *yoga* is already found in the *Vedas* and the *Upaniṣads*, in addition to being one of the six *darśanas* ('views' in relation to the *Vedas*) on which all the other types of *yoga* are largely based.[1]

Thus *yoga* has its roots in a soil that is profoundly spiritual: the soil of the *Vedas/Upaniṣads*, *darśana*.

If one had to diverge from these aspects, *yoga* would become merely a physical or mental exercise, but this would entail distorting its essence, its purpose, and its very system of ethics.

We spoke earlier of conflict; pain; the personal Divine and the impersonal Divine; *avidyā*, or ignorance, concerning the nature of Being; and *vidyā*, or knowledge, which by contrast reveals Being. Now these ideas represent the foundation on which every branch of *yoga* must be based.

If we were to ask a serious and well-prepared disciple why he practises *yoga*, he would certainly reply, 'It

[1] For a complete exposition of this topic, see *Indian Philosophy*, second volume, 'The six Brahmanical *darśanas*' by S. Radhakrishnan.

is because I recognise – as the *Vedas*, the *Upaniṣads*, and also the Western initiatory Tradition declare – that I have fallen into *avidyā* and so have forgotten my true nature. By practising *yoga* I shall overcome *avidyā* and re-integrate myself into my pure essence.'

Plato, too, says that the Soul, by coming into generation and identifying itself with it, has forgotten its intelligible or noetic nature.[1] This divine Master points to Dialectic as the supreme instrument for resolution. The *Upaniṣads* indicate various means, one of which is certainly *yoga*.

To practise *yoga*, therefore, five fundamental factors are necessary:

1. A yearning for the Divine, the Supra-sensible;
2. A vocation for one type of *yoga* or another;
3. A knowledge of the philosophical vision of *yoga*;
4. A conscious/psychological qualification;
5. An adherence to the ethics of *yoga*.

Ethics – the way of behaving – concerns the practical approach one keeps to in one's daily life. We would say that a person's ethics enables us to discern his cultural, spiritual, and aspirational level. All practise a form of ethics, including those who would deny this.

The *Yogadarśana* indicates two ethical aspects that are prerequisites to beginning the apprenticeship of *yoga* properly so called and taking up meditation. They are *yama* (self-control) and *niyama* (observances). *Yama* requires abstention from anger, deceit, theft, incontinence, and greed. *Niyama* involves purity (inner and outer), contentment/acceptance, austerity/self-discipline, study of

[1] Patañjali further states that the union of the Seer/soul with the seen/world of generation is the cause of slavery. See *The Regal Way to Realization* (*Yogadarśana*), II,17-18. Translation from the Sanskrit and commentary by Raphael. Aurea Vidyā, New York.

oneself and the teaching of *yoga*, as well as surrender and openness to the Divine.[1]

To explain the rationale behind these ethical features and their usefulness – we would say their indispensability – would require a treatise to itself, for the additional reason that it broaches technical aspects of *sādhanā* (the apprenticeship to *yoga*). It is enough to know that specific *āsanas* (postures), focus on specific *cakras*, or meditations (*dhyāna*) cause a release of energy that the *sādhaka* (disciple) is frequently unable to control, thus fuelling everything of a psychological nature (*guṇa*) that is weak, impure, inharmonious, and excessively individualised.

Through *yoga* a disciple may find himself in the paradoxical situation of seeking quietness, calmness, serenity, and supra-sensible happiness but finding super-charged energies instead which he cannot understand, master, or direct; or he may find himself in profound conflict because, while aspiring to the Divine on the one hand and setting sattvic energies in motion, he is failing on the other hand to follow a form of ethics conformable to his purpose, with the result that a struggle and conflict of energies arises, with unforeseeable consequences.

We would say that to practise *yoga*, as to do the work of a priest, a doctor, an engineer, or an artisan, one has to be *qualified*: precise qualifications or attitudes are necessary, without which we would have only bad or false *yogis*, priests, doctors, and so on.

Sometimes, especially in the West, it may come about that *yoga* is interpreted as purely physical or mental exercise for the purpose of finding merely psychological comfort because life has really reached a point of

---

1 See Patañjali, *The Regal Way to Realization* (*Yogadarśana*), II, 29 *et seqq*., op. cit.

pathological stress. But *yoga*, in its different varieties, is a means, a bridge which, if undertaken sincerely and with the right calling, leads the soul within us to the universal Soul.

HAṬHAYOGA

Haṭhayoga is based on the principle that the vital mechanism is sustained by two currents of force: the positive current corresponds to the syllable *ha*, and the negative current corresponds to the syllable *ṭha*.

When these two forces – solar and lunar, *piṅgala* and *iḍā* – are in balance, they bring the vital complex into harmony and so allow it to function perfectly. *Haṭhayoga* considers that the balance of energy which nature itself provides for the individual is defective, and so it seeks to establish another balance which will allow the physical form to sustain an increasing dynamic influx of vital force (*prāṇa*), of which unlimited quantities are found in space.

Every individual possesses a certain amount of prāṇic energy which, we might say, constitutes its energy inheritance; or rather, every individual, through particular prāṇic centres, absorbs a quantity of energy proportionate to its receiving apparatus. For an hereditary constitution, the individual is incapable of withstanding more. So, for example, a person's resistance to electrical voltage can reach a certain quota or threshold of susceptibility, but if this is exceeded he can become a victim of an electrical/molecular overload. But this does not bring us face to face with absolute values, and *Haṭhayoga* demonstrates this by opening the door to the universalisation of individual vitality and allowing the physical/prāṇic organism to receive a current of prāṇic energy that is less restricted and therefore higher than the normal amount used by the receiving apparatus.

Rather than being a philosophy or a teaching, *Haṭhayoga* is a method, a psychosomatic discipline which has two quite effective instruments as its main foundation: *āsanas* and *prāṇāyāma*.[1] The *āsanas* are the bodily 'postures', which are especially investigated with a view to favouring specific releases of energy; in addition, they bring the physical body to stillness through 'control' and 'power'. The power of physical stillness in *Haṭhayoga* is as important as the stillness or suspension of the *vṛttis* (modifications in thought) in *Rājayoga*.

It needs to be made clear that it is not a question of physical or mental 'passivity' – far from it. It is precisely in such conditions that the consciousness is more alert, more awake, more attentive, and less scattered. The activity of our mind is directed towards movement that is agitated, disordered, and capable of squandering emotional/mental energies even when it is engaged in futile matters. Those who are masters of their own thought employ only a third of the energy normally expended by an individual who cannot control his own mind. The activity of our body is also a purposeless flailing about. The dissipation of prāṇic force is enormous in daily life, whereas that energy should always be available in sufficient quantity to face up to particular contingencies, such as illness and so on. The inability to stem the flow of *prāṇa* provokes an imbalance between inflow and outflow, between the centrifugal action going outwards from the centre of the individual and the centripetal action coming from outside to the individual. Once

[1] For *prāṇāyāma* see Patañjali, *The Regal Way to Realization* (*Yogadarśana*), Chapter II,46-53, op. cit.

the equilibrium is broken, the state of energy becomes precarious and, although the receiving and transmitting apparatus is continually making adjustments, it remains conditioned and often in a poor state.

Prāṇāyāma (mastery of the breath) refers to control of the vital forces. In fact, the breath is linked to the energies of *prāṇa*, although indirectly. According to *Haṭhayoga*, *prāṇāyāma* plays a double role: on the one hand, it harmonises the inflow and outflow of the *prāṇa*, imparts greater vitality to the cell tissues, strengthens the physical body in an extraordinary way, and surpasses even the limits of its natural capacity; on the other hand, it facilitates the awakening of the *kuṇḍalini* – the prāṇic dynamism coiled in the *mūlādhāra* centre or *cakra* at the base of the spinal column – thus opening for the aspirant areas of consciousness that are unusual and certainly extraordinary.

Some of these results may manifest in what are commonly called *siddhis* (psychic powers), which do not grant true Liberation or realisation.[1] These *siddhis* are still part of the phenomenal world and in the long run they may imprison the aspirant. The question of being moves into deeper areas of awareness and requires the neophyte to aspire to goals which are necessarily more sacred and spiritual. *Samādhi* is an experience of universal order which *Haṭhayoga*, if practised intelligently under a qualified instructor, can offer in a wonderful way.

In any case, authentic *Haṭhayoga* aims, through the rise of *kuṇḍalini*, to merge *Śakti* with *Śiva* (base *cakra*

---

[1] For the psychic powers see Patañjali, *The Regal Way to Realization* (*Yogadarśana*) III,16-56; IV,1; 'The *siddhis*' in *The Pathway of Non-Duality* and 'Occultism and psychic powers' in *At the Source of Life* by Raphael. Aurea Vidyā, New York.

and head *cakra*) and then to fly from there to the transcendent state of being.[1]

In his commentary to verse 8 of the second *adhyāya* of the *Śvetaśvatara Upaniṣad*, Śaṅkara expounds the function of *prāṇāyāma*. Here is a simple note to that *sūtra*.

Prāṇāyāma – the 'control of the *prāṇa*' gained through acting upon the breath – whose purpose is the mastery and consequent equilibrium of the vital energy, has as its ultimate objective the control of the mind by means of the breath. *Prāṇa* is the vital energy, the cause of every form of dynamism and osmosis between the individual and the universe. It is not identified merely with the air, although air is one of its vehicles, or with other physical entities, for its nature is wholly subtle. In fact, whereas the act of breathing is concerned with the gross bodily part consisting of nose, mouth, bronchia, lungs, and so on, the flow of *prāṇa* occurs at the subtle level in the 'nerve channels' known as *nāḍī*. Therefore, just as the perviousness of the respiratory passage is necessary for a sufficient oxygenation of the blood, so the purification of the *nāḍīs* is necessary for the free and unhampered flow of *prāṇa*: as it spreads through the subtle structures of the various organs, it enables them to perform their activities, and the individual complex to be alive. It is *prāṇa* that makes physical life possible, by maintaining the cohesion of the vehicle. When, for various reasons – such as serious trauma, illness, the exhaustion of the organic capabilities on account of old age, and so on – the vital energy leaves the body, so, too, does the reflection of Consciousness, and the

---

[1] For the *cakras* and their alchemical correlations see the Chapter 'The Fire of Life' in *The Threefold Pathway of Fire* by Raphael, op. cit.

vehicle dies, disintegrating and allowing its component parts to return to *prakṛti*.

The practice of *prāṇāyāma* is not an essential or direct means to Knowledge, but it is an instrument that is capable of bringing the mind under control by reducing its projecting and distracting activity. *Prāṇāyāma* is practised through one or both of the nostrils and its phases are inhalation (*pūraka*), retention (*kumbhaka*), and exhalation (*recaka*). *Kumbhaka* can be inner (*antara*), subsequent to *pūraka*, or outer (*bāhya*), subsequent to *recaka*. The variations all have precise effects. It is very important to bear in mind that the exercise of *prāṇāyāma* cannot be approached in a light or superficial way or by diverting from its true purpose, which is the control of the mind. As Patañjali states in his *Yogasūtra*, *prāṇāyāma* can and must be undertaken only after consolidating the practice of the 'observances' (*yama*), the 'restrictions' (*niyama*), the 'postures' (*āsanas*) – which are also designed to restore harmony to the vehicle of the physical complex – and the 'closures' (*mudrās*) which are practised in order to avoid wasting the vital energy. It is a method of potent efficacy, and for beginners to practise it without the guidance of a competent Master who is aware of the capability and conditions of the student conceals many pitfalls. Thus it may be found to be quite dangerous, especially if it is not directed to the mastery of the mind and its final solution. In the absence of these essential prerequisites, one is left with a storehouse of energies that lacks the competence which is indispensable for giving them direction, and with the risk of losing control of them at the nervous level, the mental level, and even the organic level.[1]

---

[1] See Śaṅkara, *Aparokṣānubhūti* 118-120, edited by Raphael. Aurea Vidyā, New York.

KARMAYOGA

Karmayoga is the pathway of 'actionless action', or detachment from the fruits of action. This involves determining oneself through an act of pure action without attachment. The ordinary individual acts because he is moved by the desire to possess: the follower of this path acts without the desire to receive. This is the *yoga* of action (*karma*) that is taught by the *Bhagavadgītā*.

> 'O Anagha [Arjuna], as I have told you before, there are twin paths in this world: one is related to *Sāṁkhyayoga*, whose means is knowledge (*jñāna*), and the other is related to *Karmayoga*, whose means is action.
>
> 'Not by rejecting action will man attain freedom from acting; nor by merely abandoning [all action] will he reach the perfection of *Samādhi*.
>
> 'No one can remain without acting, even for an instant, for he is inexorably driven to action by the qualities (*guṇas*) of *prakṛti*.
>
> 'A man who, even while controlling the organs of action (*karmendriya*), continues to think of sense objects is said to be deluded and hypocritical.
>
> 'By contrast, O Arjuna, a man who, restraining the senses by means of the mind and having no attachment, undertakes *Karmayoga* through the means of action is victorious [over the others].

'Fulfil, then, the action that is due, because action is better than inactivity [inertia]; without action it would not even be possible to keep your body alive.

'Except for action based on sacrifice [non-binding action], the world is bound to action, O Kaunteya. Therefore perform action as a sacrifice and be free of attachment.'[1]

It is obvious that this kind of action does not originate from the realm of the individual and is not directed to the individual and particular. The disciple's skill in this kind of *yoga* consists in allowing the empirical ego to die, together with its contents of possessions and acquisitions, and in merging with the Principle for universal purposes. This is the *yoga* for people of action, whose urges are directed to acting in the various fields of human activity. In this way the disciple becomes an instrument of the divine will by supporting the process of becoming and embracing its rhythms and its ways of working.

In the *Gītā*, Kṛṣṇa continually exhorts his disciple to take refuge in him, to be united with him, to find identity with him; and his insistence is undoubtedly necessary, for the action of *Karmayoga* requires the salutary impetus of complete dedication, faithfulness, and devotion to the will of universal Being. In the struggle for the ideal and the just cause, the neophyte effects the 'breaking of the ego's level' through the force of sacrifice, whereas the *jñāni* completes this rupture by means of discrimination, discernment, and intellective intuition. On one side, there is a striving upwards; on the other side, with the *jñāni*, an intuitive recognition of what one really is. On the one hand, there are action

[1] See *Bhagavadgītā* (The Celestial Song), III,3-9. Translation from the Sanskrit and commentary by Raphael. Aurea Vidyā, New York.

and fire which break through and consume; on the other hand, there are silence and contemplation which are full of revelatory sounds.

> '*Karma-Yoga* is thus an ethical and religious method whose purpose is to re-unite us with freedom by means of altruism and good actions. The *karma-yogi* has no need to believe in any doctrine. He may even not believe in God, wonder what his soul might be, or be attached to any speculation of a metaphysical order. His essential aim is to free himself from egoism and do so through his own strength ...
>
> 'Thus the only solution is to renounce all the fruits of action and be detached from it ... When a man can do this, he will be a Buddha and will find within himself the strength to work in a way that will transform the world. Such a man represents the highest ideal of *Karma-Yoga*.'[1]

We need to appreciate Movement that requires no movement, Action that requires no action, just as we need to appreciate that Love which requires no love. Can Love desire love if it is itself love? Can the sun desire light if it itself is light?

When we can express ourselves as action without attraction or attachment, the egoistic 'I' is resolved and remains pure Action, pure Movement, pure Being, pure Love.

The West, with its frenzied pursuit of activity, its tendency to be extrovert, and its continuous 'doing', should practise this healthy kind of *yoga*. Relations between individuals and nations would quickly change, finally bringing harmony to human contacts. The psychological

---

[1] Vivekānanda, *Karma-Yoga*, Chapter 'The ideal of *Karma-Yoga*'.

and physical attitude of non-violence is the essential feature of *Karmayoga*.[1]

---

[1] For a deeper understanding of *Karmayoga* see *Bhagavadgītā*, op. cit.

BHAKTIYOGA

The *yoga* of devotion and love raises its sphere of operation from the physical plane, where *Haṭhayoga* is established, to the plane of emotion and feelings. This is the *yoga* that is practised with the heart, with transformed feeling, with steady, constant devotion to the God-Person. We may say that this is the way that is most followed and most experienced. The principle of *Bhaktiyoga* is to make use of the normal ties of life, which are characterised by the play of emotions, in order to 'avail oneself' of the Beloved. Meditation and rituals themselves serve solely to enhance the intensity of the divine contact.

The individual has always turned to a God in order to prostrate himself and ask for his help. It is an innate human need to feel protected, to *abandon oneself* to the power of the Divine, and to feel fulfilled.

The Sanskrit word *Bhakti* comes from the root *bhaj*, which means 'pay homage', 'worship', 'serve', and therefore to place oneself at the service of the Godhead with total dedication and self-denial. The disciple who adopts this 'approach' to the Divine continually expands his feelings until he actually feels the Godhead within himself. This is the pathway for those whose love of God is felt so intensely that they turn their backs on all other worldly allurements. Only love and great devotion for the Beloved can shake these disciples, inflamed as they are with divine frenzy. Their immense capacity for 'being absorbed' means that the Master, the Teacher, or the cosmic Beloved become the objects of profound, tenacious adoration that is truly felt. The disciple worships his own Teacher, his own Soul (the inner Teacher), the divine Teacher, according to his own level of consciousness. With every step that is taken on this pathway, individuality loses some of its content and significance. For His sake, for the sake of the divine Beloved, everything can perish, even life if need be.[1]

Radhakrishnan says, 'For those who defend the way of devotion other-worldly redemption matters less than absolute submission to the unchanging will of God.'[2]

For love of the Father the devoted are able to love all that the Father loves: 'Father, thy Will, not mine, be done.'[3]

It is their great thirst for devotion which urges them on to the peak of the extreme thrust of aspiration, with the result that their inner fires are sufficiently kindled to produce a great flame, which, extending towards the heart of the Beloved, raises their consciousness to unparalleled divine ecstasy. The consummation is the possession of God; total self-denial lets the Divine come forth. God works in them, because they give themselves totally to God. The bridegroom or the bride of the Lord of love becomes so exalted as to partake of that heavenly wedding-feast which is the tangible sign of the loss of oneself as a separate individuality.

Here is the exclamation of a great *bhakta*:

> 'He speaks to me and tells me that I am his. My Lord, my Christ, you are mine and I am yours. You

---

[1] See Śaṅkara, *Vivekacūḍāmaṇi*, 'Personal effort and Guru', 31 *et seqq.*, op. cit.

[2] S. Radhakrishnan, *Bhagavadgītā*, 'Introduction', op.cit.

[3] St Luke, 22:42; St Mark, 14:36; St Matthew, 26:39.

are my life. This heart, this mind, this Soul, I lay at your feet. I love you, I love you!'

And again, in the *Bhāgavata* (III, 25,33) we read:

'Before knowledge can arise, the fact of finding oneself in duality can be distracting, but when our mind is made clear, we can be aware that duality is more beautiful than Non-duality and that it exists so that an act of worship can take place ... The truth is Non-duality, but duality exists for the provision of worship; and so worship itself is a hundred times greater than liberation.'[1]

The *bhakta* is one who – in deep devotion, tenderness, piety, love, and compassion – 'submits' himself to the Lord. Only the indisputable giving of oneself to the Beloved can result in the Beloved's taking care of the lover.

Madhusūdana defines *Bhakti* as that condition of the spirit in which the spirit itself, being drawn by an ecstasy of love, assumes the form of the Godhead.

On other paths, there is the conviction that man himself, through an act of volition, has to raise himself to the Divine, with the result that there is an 'ascent', whereas in *Bhakti* it is God that has to come down into the human being, and hence there is a 'descent'. The individual simply has to empty himself of all the psychological contents, so that the Lord may descend and save him through grace.

Bhakti is divided into *aparabhakti* and *parabhakti*, that is, non-supreme and supreme *Bhakti*. *Aparabhakti* concerns the 'Lesser Mysteries' and operates at the level of purification, the activation of ethical qualities, psychological harmonisations, and so on. *Parabhakti* operates

---

[1] S. Radhakrishnan, *Bhagavadgītā*, 'Introduction', p. 77, op. cit.

at the level of self-transfiguration until one attains the 'perfection of the Father' and identity with Him.

If this terminology is accepted, *aparabhakti* may be said to be exoteric, while *parabhakti* is esoteric. The former expresses itself at the individual level, both particular and general, and the latter at the noetic level of the universal or the Principle. It may also be said that the former is concerned with ascetical theology, the latter with pure mysticism.

As we have seen, the word *Bhakti* means participation, devotion, surrender; and surrender/devotion happens through love (*prema*). *Bhakti* is therefore the giving of oneself to the Father through love.

> 'God is love; and he that dwelleth in love dwelleth in God, and God in him.'
>
> 'But he that is joined unto the Lord is one spirit.'[1]

Like all ways of spiritual discipline, *Bhaktiyoga* has stages, ways of working, and its own ways of looking at the paths. Since it is *yoga* of a practical nature, all it can do is to indicate a precise and definite *sādhanā* (discipline/ascesis).

For the convenience of Christians in the West, the *sādhanā* described is that of *Premayoga*, the *yoga* of Love. The *sādhanā* proposed here, however, omits the purely theological postulates of Christianity, and forgiveness is asked for anything that is not in harmony with these postulates. For obvious reasons we shall have to allude to the general principles which shape the *sādhanā* itself.

In the Garden of Eden (the Hindu *brahmaloka*) are located the Tree of life or the *aśvattha* (unity) and the Tree of the knowledge of good and evil (becoming or

---

[1] I John, 4:16; I Corinthians, 6:17.

saṁsāra in Buddhism). Through an act of free will, primordial Adam experiences the fruits of this imprisoning duality, to escape from which he has to rediscover himself and realise his identity with the Tree of life or truth.

Christ came to give 'the keys of the Kingdom of Heaven', that is, the teaching that effects liberation. In the Gospels we read,

> 'And the disciples came, and said unto him, Why speakest thou unto them in parables? He answered and said unto them, because it is given unto you to know the mysteries of the kingdom of heaven, but to them it is not given.'[1]

Jesus embodied the Principle of love, which is consubstantial with the Father.

> 'No man cometh unto the Father, but by me.'[2]

Love is therefore the key to open those gates which have been closed through choosing to experience duality (the Tree of the knowledge of good and evil). When the extroverted polar desire is resolved into unitive love for the Tree of life, then Adam returns to being the pure undivided Spirit.

If original sin, or the 'fall',[3] has provoked the scissure between man and God, or a great space, Love/the Son, born of the universal Father/Mary, reduces this space until it is eliminated. Love is the opposite of egotism, the egotism which has created the scissure. Rejection of unity and attachment to multiplicity, to the particular, and to the individual have led Adam to sunder

---

1 St Matthew, 13:10-11.

2 St John, 14:6.

3 For the 'fall', see 'The "fall" of the Soul' in *The Pathway of Non-Duality*, and 'Original Sin and Christianity' in *Beyond Doubt*, by Raphael. Aurea Vidyā, New York.

himself from the All and establish himself as a part – an individual among individuals – in opposition to the principle. *Vedānta* declares that from the *buddhi* is produced *ahaṁkāra*, 'the sense of I' or egoicity. Christ has 'anchored' on the earth a universal principle which must be grasped, assimilated, lived, and expressed by that fallen Adam who wishes to return to the 'primordial state'.

Love may be interpreted esoterically or exoterically, and the vision changes according to the way one views love.

In general the human race has interpreted love in terms of egotistic feeling and desire, while love – it is worth repeating – is a universal principle, as are will and intelligence. By humanising and anthropomorphising God/Christ, we have 'brought Him down' to the level of merely emotional feeling, and emotion, being principally a feature of the ego, goes looking, as we know, for gratification and psychological comfort.

A philosophy, a religion, a political conception, and so on, can arise in order to satisfy the ego and give it comfort rather than attempting to resolve it and transcend it.

Initiation into the Mysteries of Love

The '*yoga* of love' (*Premayoga*) can be succinctly presented in five stages, or *aṇgas*, as evinced by Christ Himself:

- Baptism/purification
- Transfiguration
- 'Crucifixion' or 'death' of the individualised
- Ascension
- Union

These events in the life of Jesus may be understood at the *apara* level or the *para* level, from the exoteric viewpoint or the esoteric viewpoint. *Premayoga* has affinities with *parabhakti*. It is merely a question of remembering that the five *aṇgas* listed above can be correlated to the eight steps of Patañjali's *Rājayoga*.[1]

The first two stages are preparations for the 'death of the ego', the ego that is born from experiencing the Tree of the knowledge of good and evil. Purification entails the elimination of all those discords which obscure and veil the vibration of Love/the Principle: the love which has always resonated because it represents the Father Himself, but which the fallen Adam has transformed into a lower octave that is individualised and degraded, into desire and self-love. It is therefore necessary to

---

[1] See *The Regal Way to Realization* (*Yogadarśana*), II,29 *et seqq.*, op. cit.

recapture the original vibration, which means capturing that primordial sound which 'moves the sun and the other stars'.[1]

Purification or the 'baptism by fire' – so called because it burns away all the dross deposited in the psychosomatic constitution – is followed by transfiguration, which transforms individuality, making it transparent, completely innocent, and *luminous* (this word is not used symbolically).

This state of consciousness, profoundly re-orientated towards the glory of the Principle, leads to the crucifixion or *death* of the egoistic/individual complex in its entirety. Adam's nature, which has been patiently nurtured, is shattered, and in the desert, where there are no projections or supports, the consciousness hears the sound of love that seizes, attracts, and sublimates.

> 'No one is full of God unless he is constantly dead to himself, stripped of himself in God.'[2]

> 'Father, into thy hands I commend my spirit.'[3]

The ascension is *flying* – because the being has been made light by the earlier stages – towards the living love as the essential reality: 'Yet not I, but Christ liveth in me.'[4] It represents the rapture of the lover for the Beloved, the consummation of the heavenly marriage. The consciousness resorts more and more to the very source of love until there is a point of fusion, union. In this ocean, where paeans of love resound with praise, consciousness creates identity with the Word:

---

[1] Dante, *Paradise*, XXXIII,145.

[2] Meister Eckhart, *Treatises and sermons*: 'The Book of Divine Consolation', page 123. Rusconi, Milano 1982.

[3] St Luke, 23:46.

[4] Galatians, 2:20.

'I and my Father are one ... He that seeth me seeth the Father.'[1]

'Neither pray I for these alone, but for them also which shall believe in me through their word; that they all may be one; as thou, Father, art in me, and I in thee, that they also may be one in us ... I in them, and thou in me, that they may be made perfect in one.'[2]

The first three stages are active, and the being takes itself by the hand:

'Draw nigh to God, and he will draw nigh to you.'[3]

The final two stages are ones of surrender and offering: the being lets itself be taken. To draw nigh to the expressive power of the Word means letting oneself be engulfed and absorbed, like a heavenly body which comes too close to the sun's centre of gravity.

The being becomes free only when it has succeeded in eliminating from itself whatever initially alienated and distanced it from the Principle/the Father, in whom 'we live, and move, and have our being.' [Acts, 17:28]. The key to enable this process of liberation is love, and the *yoga* of love is the raft/the *sādhanā* for crossing the ocean of bondage. Initiation into the mystery of the Kingdom of love leads the neophyte to become one with those that *are*.

---

[1] St John, 10:30, 12:45.

[2] *Ibid.* 17:20-21-23.

[3] Epistle of James, 4:8.

Baptism/Purification

With regard to purification (*yama* and *niyama*, the first two *aṅgas* of *Rājayoga*), there are several techniques. We shall briefly examine just three, which are mere moments of a single operation.

The first enhances the internalisation of the centre of consciousness so as to be able to create a 'distance' from the whole of the psychic world of reaction.

The second acts by means of a *mantra* (a monosyllabic sound) which has an ultrasonic force sufficient to dissolve the subconscious contents.

The third promotes the stabilisation of the point at the centre of consciousness as a preparation for further steps.

Through these three movements, the embodied reflection of consciousness is moved from the periphery of its psychosomatic constitution to the centre. The discordant sounds of the lower nature are weakened and gradually dispelled. Reactive individuality comes to silence, thereby yielding itself to the fire of transfiguration.

Purification entails not only the empowering of moral qualities (subjective and psychological morality) but also the *transformation* of the vibrational state of the individuality as a whole. Psychosomatic individuality is a vibrating complex which can sound harmony or disharmony: an emotional current charged with hatred, for example, creates a state of vibration which influences the surrounding space. Those with a practised eye can detect certain disturbances produced in the environment.

In the work of purification, individuality cannot be taken to its 'correct firing' and cannot begin the phase of transfiguration and the consequent 'crucifixion', or *death*, of the whole Adamitic complex without the intervention of boldness, discrimination, detachment (*vairāgya*), and so on. 'Neither do men put new wine into old bottles.'[1] At this first stage the *mantra* plays its part as the element that resolves the subconscious accretions.

Man is constrained by the gravitational power of his own crystallised, petrified, and solidified world (*vāsanā*). A psychic content is a coagulation of energy shot through with a particular tendency (*saṁskāra*). It is a piece of ice which needs to be restored to a liquid state; mass has to be transformed into energy.[2]

Within the being, there is often a duality between the deliberating consciousness of the moment and the subconscious content. The consciousness considers acting in a certain way, but the subconscious opposes and often defeats the consciousness.

> 'For if we have been planted together in the likeness of his death, we shall be also in the likeness of his resurrection: knowing this, that our old man is crucified with him, that the body of sin might be destroyed, that henceforth we should not serve sin. For he that is dead is freed from sin.'[3]

> 'For that which I do I allow not; for what I would, that do I not; but what I hate, that I do ... for to will is present with me; but how to perform that

---

1 St Matthew, 9:17.

2 To go deeper into these aspects, see: 'The origin of subconsciousness' in *Tat tvam asi* (You are That) by Raphael and 'Solution of the coagulates of energy' in *Beyond the illusion of the ego* by Raphael. Aurea Vidyā, New York.

3 Romans, 6:5-7.

which is good I find not ... I find then a law, that, when I would do good, evil is present with me.'[1]

'Walk in the Spirit, and ye shall not fulfil the lust of the flesh. For the flesh lusteth against the Spirit, and the Spirit against the flesh: and these are contrary the one to the other: so that ye cannot do the things that ye would.'[2]

The battle must be engaged with intelligence, with adequate preparation, and with appropriate incentives, but it is a battle that has to be waged and it is the duty of each to wage it. Although every manoeuvre is always supported by the grace of divine love, it is still the individual who needs to operate at certain levels; if he does not, he may fall into quietism, sterile passivity, total inertia. It would be too convenient for the ego to hand over to the divine power the task of lifting him forcibly from the hell into which he has driven himself. In the preliminary phases it is essential to look out for any specious reasoning that the ego might put forward.

With intelligent action from the individual and the love of the all-pervading principle, the victory cannot but be won: 'Be of good cheer; I have overcome the world.'[3]

---

[1] *Ibid.* 7:15 *et seqq.*

[2] Galatians, 5:16-17.

[3] St John, 16:33.

Transfiguration

As the process moves forward, step by step, of solving the subconscious vibrational conglomeration (crystallised evil/egoism in opposition to Good/Love), the phase of transfiguration has already begun.

During the operational *iter*, however, the consciousness, now freed from the burden and vibrational disharmony of the first Adam, is ready to begin sounding a different *mantra*, which represents a harmonic of the note of universal love and has to be sounded in the centre that is designed to open within us that 'window' which is appropriate for the level of life in which we wish to operate. Love can begin to germinate in the heart when egotism has released its grip. One cannot love while remaining egoistic; one cannot know while remaining ignorant.

The work of transfiguration entails profound internalisation, solitude, and mental silence. It is a question of knowing how to tune the 'ear' to the subtle, hyper-physical musicality of the inner Christ. This is also the work of invoking, evoking, precipitating, and stabilising the universal sound in one's own heart. It should be stated that Christ sounded the note of love at three levels of existence: causal, manifest universal (subtle), and physical/gross, by means of the sounded word. The two notes of the physical and the subtle (the gross and the hyper-physical manifestation) are *harmonics* of the fundamental note, which is the immortal Word on its own plane (*śabdabrahman*).

Step by step the human constitution is transformed and consciousness *comprehends* that reality itself, in its essential and noetic basis, cannot be conceived in terms of empirical knowledge and subject/object. Rational discriminations, like conceptual definitions, disappear, because they have lost their motive and purpose. Thought suffers the setback of its own failure to recognise – above its being and its level of operation – the innocent and joyous beauty of limitless love with its inherent aspect of wisdom. Thought, the longing to learn via the senses, the anguish experienced when confronting humiliating and paralysing impotence: all fall silent, because in the end they are swept away by the *pax profunda*, in which all thoughts and words become absurd emptiness.

The soul finds itself suspended between two extremes: the One/the Father, which stands above everything, and the negativity of the Adamitic nature, the begetter of chaos and dark rebellion. But love/wisdom, which now penetrates and enlightens the centre of the re-orientated soul, bestows on it the certainty that the source of its sublimity and transcendence can be found not outside itself, but ever more within itself. This implies that the two *cakras* or centres – the heart centre (*anāhata*) and the centre between the eyebrows (*ājñā*) – are harmonising, co-ordinating, and integrating with each other. The mind and the heart are merging; love is pervaded by wisdom, and wisdom by love. At the same time the centre at the top of the head, the *sahasrāra* – the synthesis of all the *cakras* and seat of the transcendent Spirit – begins to be activated.

On the mount of divine transfiguration, *avidyā* (metaphysical ignorance) loses its focus before being inexorably dispelled by the joyous rays of love/wisdom, the power which finds fulfilment as the peace and joy which are commensurate with the Divine. In this state of consciousness, the soul no longer seeks to enjoy external or profane events, but ardently yearns for unchanging identity with the Spirit. When the soul is able to check the outward movement of its powers, it flows back to its primordial state of wholeness, relishing the joy and delight of harmony, love, and wisdom.

> 'These things ... have been extolled by our noble teacher [Hierotheus] in his theological *Elements*: whether he learned them from the sacred writers or discovered them from scientific investigation of the scriptures after exercising himself in them and practising them for a long time, or whether he was initiated by a more divine inspiration after learning divine matters and then experiencing them and – if we may put it like this – becoming perfect on account of his affinity with them in unity and secret faith.'[1]

---

[1] Dionysius the Areopagite, *The Divine Names*, II, 9, 648 b. Rusconi, Milano 1981.

Crucifixion/Death

This imponderable movement of return, of penetration into the deep abysses of life, leads individuality to the *death*, the crucifixion, of the *natured*[1], the multiple, all that becomes and is subject to dispersal.

Father Philipon writes as follows:

> 'While the gift of knowledge/science[2] takes an ascending movement to raise the souls of creatures even to God, while the gift of intellect, with a mere glance of love, penetrates all the mysteries of God within and without, the gift of Wisdom never departs, so to speak, from the very heart of the Trinity. Everything is seen from this indivisible Centre ... It is the glance of the Word that breathes Love ... Taken into the fathomless abyss of the Divine Person, as if into their innermost life, the soul that has been deified under the impulse of the Spirit of Love contemplates everything from this height.'[3]

Christ is seen no longer in a static (physical form) but in a dynamic, operational (subtle) form; no longer

---

[1] *Natura Naturata - Natura Naturans*: these two terms are from Scholastic philosophy; they are also used by St Thomas Aquinas, philosopher, mystic, and theologian. 'Natured' concerns nature which is already in manifestation (gross and subtle states); 'naturing' refers to the principial level.

[2] Science: *Philos*. In the sense of 'Knowledge' as opposed to 'belief' or 'opinion'. The Compact Edition Of The Oxford English Dictionary.

[3] M. Philipon, O.P., *Sister Elisabeth's spiritual doctrine of the Trinity*, quoted by Father A. Royo Marin in *Theology of Christian perfection*. San Paolo Edizioni, Torino 2003.

external, but within one's own dimensionless awareness; no longer as one to be worshipped, but as one to be *revealed*. While this process is happening and catharsis is taking place, the sound/*mantra* is assimilated to the sound/note of Christ and is transformed into the subtle note of love.

The being perceives that it is only a vibration of love, not an individuality with bodies, and not a *particular* being. It is only vibrating love, because Christ is a cohesive sound, a harmonious tonal accord revealing total comprehension, the centre of the universe, the fundamental note resonating in space (*ākāśa*), the *mantra* that sings *Hosannah*. What is conceived as Christ becomes the authentic divine Word which, with its rhythm, harmonises the spheres of life. All beings must be seen as comprising a close-meshed web, with geometric points of light which create perfect symmetries. Love creates harmony of proportions, makes space assonant and the geometric points commensurate.

Before this level is reached, however, it is necessary to pay great attention to whatever is perceived: sounds, forms, and colours without form. That which faces us is always a second that has no absolute reality. It is not a question of seeing or going outside ourselves, but of *being*. It is not a question of observing the form/likeness/image of Christ, but of *being* a Christ-like vibration of love.

Ascension and Union

Love, in short, is released by instinct, by emotion/feeling, and by psychic conceptualisations. By going back to being a pure movement of the Spirit, unconditioned by the influence of the individualised, it discovers its *freedom*, for love, as pure spiritual essence, is true freedom, whereas desire is a prison.

Love gives freedom because it is freedom; desire gives bondage because it itself is bondage. To detach the energy of love from all the superimpositions of concept, feeling, and instinct means, furthermore, that love no longer *clings* to objective aspects, whatever their natures and degrees. Love for the Principle is not simply for mine, yours, his, or hers, and is not conditioned by a particular creed, for if it were, it would cling to the individual, the selective, the exclusive, and such moments are those of desire.

Love is like the wind, which 'bloweth where it listeth'; it is like the sun, which shines on the just and the unjust, the saints and the sinners.

'Love your enemies, and pray for them which persecute you, that ye may be children of your Father which is in heaven; for he maketh his sun to rise on the evil and on the good, and sendeth rain on the just and on the unjust.'[1]

---

1 St Matthew, 5:44-45.

Love that is released from the fetters of profane and spiritual passions shines with a light that is not contaminated by the dialectic of the mind/*manas*.

In *savikalpa samādhi*, the being transcends name and form and *ascends*, being absorbed by the powerful, original, and causal vibration of love. A merging takes place, as when a river joins one that is larger and realises itself as a unity with it. This *samādhi* reveals love as it manifests on the various planes of existence. Though it is a unity, it comprehends the apparent multiplicity expressed by the fundamental Note.

That *mantra*/sound which had been used in the earlier phases is no longer *heard* at the gross level or at the subtle level, because now one is the very essence of the universal sound, which has resolved into the Word, which pervades and vitalises everything. The soul itself has dissolved into pure Spirit: 'But he that is joined unto the Lord is one spirit [with Him].'[1]

An *avatāra* is the embodiment of a divine Principle that reveals itself through a temporary form at some specific level of existence.

Christ did not come to comfort the psyche of the fallen Adam. He did not come to support the lazy or to place on the altar the emotional sufferings of men, but to restore the erring son to the Father by means of initiation into Mysteries of Christly love: an initiation which entails *purification*, *transfiguration*, *crucifixion*, *ascension*, and *union*.

These initiatory stages can be realised through the *yoga* of love (*Premayoga*), the *yoga* of resolving Fire.

---

[1] I Corinthians, 6:17.

RAJAYOGA

Rājayoga (royal *yoga*), codified by Patañjali in his *Yogasūtra*[1], has as its end the suspension/solution of the modifications of the mind (*citta-vṛtti-nirodha*). When this has been effected and stabilised, then the Seer (pure consciousness, *puruṣa*, or the real being) is established on its true nature, which implies that it is no longer determined by the movement of *prakṛti/substance/nature.*

What are the 'modifications of the mind'? They are the unending impulses, ideations, projections, extroverted movements of the mind, and these movements are, in their turn, nothing but the effects of a cause which is further upstream and which represents what we call *desire.* Desire impels the substance of mind to move, to determine itself, and also to find the means of attaining satisfaction and gratification. Desire represents a disturbance of the equilibrium, an infringement of a pre-established order.

But why do we desire? It is because we do not know our authentic nature, because we have *forgotten* what we really are, and so we are constrained to chase feverishly after some object of desire. Once we have obscured or covered over our true being, which *is* and does not become, it is clear that we have to be content with substitutes, with things which, however much apparent gratification and satisfaction they grant, can

[1] See *The Regal Way to Realization* (*Yogadarśana*), op. cit.

never replace the nature of being, which is fullness or objectless bliss.

And what are we really? According to the *Yogasūtra* (and the whole of the Vedic/Mystery initiatory Tradition), we are immortal beings, self-radiant beings; we are *puruṣas* (universal Persons); we are eternal souls which 'are what they are'; we are the self-existent *ātman*, which depends on nothing and on no 'second'.

And how do we recognise this immortal nature of ours? It is definitely not by merely conceptualising in the mind or by creating further illusory *vṛttis*, but by effecting the *Yogasūtra*, that is, by actually suspending the 'modifications of the mind'. Through this empirical practice we reach the essence of what we really are. By putting a stop to the process of becoming within us, we reveal Being. For example, how do we discover hydrogen, which is the simplest of the elements? By breaking down the chemical compound until we actually reach the essence of what chemical compounds are. In the human realm there are geniuses who have intuited, theorised, and formulated certain truths (and these are the true pioneers); and there are others who wish to experience 'empirically' those truths that have been formulated.

Yoga, in its true connotation (and apart from all the deformations that it has undergone and continues to undergo, to the point where the very term *yoga* almost needs modifying), is the empirical, pragmatic, and operative aspect for revealing that fundamental truth which it enunciates. Understood in this way, *yoga* is an 'experiential vision', both theory and practice: these two aspects have to be integrated if we wish to obtain the right result. *Yoga* can tell you that you are the immortal and supreme lord of yourself and also give you the practical, working means to demonstrate and reveal this truth.

Many people are deliberately agnostic and unconditional in their denial. The motivations for being so may be so numerous and varied that there is no point in going into them and straying from our present objective of synthesis. If *yoga* maintains that the 'modifications of the mind' (*vṛttis*) can be checked, suspended, and even transcended, it also provides the means for the practical realisation of this proposition; and if there are some who, for particular reasons, do not succeed, this is not to say that others, who possess the right qualifications, are bound to fail.

If, then, desire is deprivation, a lack of something, and a need, this means that our consciousness is identified with something relative, dependent, with something which is not *causa sui*, which is not its own foundation. And it is obvious that whatever is not founded upon itself must of necessity find completion and satisfaction in something other than itself. This identification of the conscious reflection of the *puruṣa* with transitory and unstable aspects is named *avidyā* by *yoga*.

Avidyā means taking the temporal, the contingent, and the relative to be the Absolute, taking the unreal to be the real (*Yogasūtra*, II, 5). Thus *avidyā*, being the cause of identification with the unreal, is the root of all the *kleśa*s (afflictions) which Patañjali deals with in Chapter II, *śloka* 3 *et seqq.* Whatever is visible, objective, and manifest in *prakṛti* represents the contingent, the relative, non-being, the world of names and forms which comes and goes, appears and disappears, and is subject to duality/polarity, while *the one who* sees is the witness or the immortal *puruṣa*. What has to be avoided is the *identification* of the witness with what it witnessed (II, 17).

From these *śloka*s we can understand that *avidyā*, as the cause of a darkening and a forgetting of oneself, compels the creation of a false self/ego (*Asmitā*, the feeling of individuality, that is the feeling of 'I am this separate self/ego'), which, because it is not founded upon itself, creates attachment/attraction towards something and consequently aversion/repulsion. The ego, being thus driven from one pole to the other (pleasure, pain), is compelled to seek for experiences (*abhiniveśas*), deceiving itself with the hope of finding satisfaction and happiness. But pleasure/pain, being typical of the world of names and forms, is a two-sided coin, with one side including the other; or rather, according to Patañjali, pleasure itself – by the mere fact of being a substitute and a factor that is undoubtedly transient – already bears pain within itself. Being tossed from one pole of existence to the other is a matter of everyday experience for all of us.

Avidyā constrains us to see the immortal as mortal, the absolute as relative, and the unreal as real. Thus the being, under the effect of *avidyā* (and therefore believing itself to be, for example, the physical body/vehicle), thinks itself to be mortal, dependent, in need, in duality, and so on, with all the consequences that can stem from this view or belief. Whatever is visible (which therefore includes the gross physical body and all the other bodies possessed by the being) is merely a means, a *medium* by which the *puruṣa* is able to reveal itself, to manifest itself, be apparent. Acquiring the visible of every order and level, even by violence, is the result of believing it to be the source of absolute necessity, of happiness, of gratification, when in fact it proves itself to be alienation, conflict, and suffering. Through this distorted view truth comes to be turned on its head: the visible becomes real/absolute, and the seer/witness becomes a subordinate effect, even, at times, disregarded and rejected.

The false and deceptive 'I' becomes true and real. The Self, the *puruṣa*, the *ātman*, the 'real Man', the witness, becomes unreal. But *prakṛti*/the visible is a mere instrument for the witness (II, 21), or, rather, the visible disappears completely (is integrated and transcended) for those who are liberated, while it continues to exist for those who still have to be liberated (II, 22). In fact, the dispersal or solution of the assimilation of the witness to the visible, the product of *avidyā*, is the certain remedy and represents its liberation (II, 25).

In order to realise the detachment of the witness from the visible, the *Yogasūtra*, contrary to what might be thought, points out various effective means: surrender to *Īśvara*, *viveka*/*vairāgya*, and the eight *aṇgas* (means).

Surrender to Īśvara

Surrender to *Īśvara* concerns *bhakti* (devotion/love), and so the *Yogasūtra* includes *bhakti* as well. Patañjali speaks of the surrender to *Īśvara* in *pāda* I, *śloka* 23, and in *pāda* II, *ślokas* 32 and 45.

What does *Īśvara* represent? *Īśvara* is the supreme *Puruṣa* untouched by the various contingent afflictions and unaffected by actions and their results (I, 24). The *Yoga* of Patañjali, being a *darśana*, is based on the *Vedas* and the *Upaniṣads*. It is thus within the context of the pure vedic/upaniṣadic Tradition, and much of it is linked to *Sāṁkhya*, which is another *darśana*. So, within the traditional context, *Īśvara* is that supreme *Puruṣa* whose various existing *puruṣas* are none other than his 'moments of consciousness'. Now, surrender to *Īśvara* entails considering ourselves no longer as separate and sundered beings but as integrating parts of the unity of *Īśvara*. Hence we have the word *yoga*, which connotes joining, unifying, reintegrating, merging the particular into the universal, 'this' individual into the universal *That*.

Rājayoga thus represents the means by which the separate individual becomes once more the universal unity, because the nature of the being is universal; it is divine unity; it is the unity of the supra-sensible consciousness. The fulfilment/perfection of *Samādhi*, which, in the final analysis, is none other than the 'suspension of the modifications of the mind' in its totality, can therefore be realised through surrender to *Īśvara* (*Īśvarapraṇidhānāt*,

II, 45). How? *Citta-vṛttis* are caused by *avidyā*, and the *vṛttis* give rise to attachment to the visible. Now if this powerful energy/love/yearning/*eros* towards what is seen outwardly is redirected towards the transcendent *Īśvara*, or our divine counterpart, there naturally occurs a total conversion, a re-orientation of consciousness, a detachment from the conflictual visible, and one is established no longer on 'this' (*asmitā*) but on That. In other words, if the desire for *things* is transmuted into love, this restores the wings to the 'fallen' *puruṣa*, thus enabling it to fly towards its divine essence. It represents Plato's *Eros*, which manifests as 'thirst for the Divine' and no longer as thirst for the things that ... are not.[1]

The thirst of the *puruṣa* which believes itself to be individualised (*asmitā*, 'I am this', II, 6) can be extinguished only by drinking of a water that can quench the thirst for all eternity: this is the Vedic *soma*. *Īśvarapraṇidhana* creates *paravairāgya*, supreme detachment, shatters the bondage to contingent desires, resolves the conflictual *cittavṛttis*, and the lover/*puruṣa* merges with the beloved *Parapuruṣa* (supreme *Puruṣa*).

---

[1] See 'Platonic Ascent: the ascent of the philosophical Eros' in *Initiation into the Philosophy of Plato*, by Raphael. Aurea Vidyā, New York.

Viveka/Vairāgya

Viveka/vairāgya was mentioned earlier as another *yogic* means of realisation. For those who have developed discrimination/discernment (*viveka*), everything turns out to be conflict/suffering (II, 15). If intuitive discernment brings us to recognise that the relative and dualistic visible is not the ultimate reality, then this visible will never be able to grant steadfast bliss or steady knowledge; and so it follows that conscious detachment (*vairāgya*), and not just formal detachment, from the conflictual visible cannot but lead to being what one is.

Viveka and *vairāgya* are thus the two distinctive techniques of the *darśana* of *Vedānta*.

> 'Non-attachment (*vairāgya*) is the conscious mastery of those who have ceased to thirst for visible and audible objects.'
>
> 'That supreme [detachment] is [also] represented by total freedom from the *guṇas* as a result of the *puruṣa*'s act of consciousness.'[1]

Non-attachment or detachment – if it is not to be an enforced falling back upon oneself – must be based upon intuitive discernment, the discrimination between that which is eternal, immortal, absolute, and that which is not; between that which is Being, inasmuch as it *is* and does not become, and that which is mere appearance, substitution, accident. Thus *viveka* is the fruit of

[1] *The Regal Way to Realization*, I.15-16, op. cit.

knowledge (*jñāna*), or gnosis, which is able to reveal the ultimate, real nature of things. And when cognitive discernment shows that phenomenon/appearance, though participating in the reality of being, is not reality as such, then the reflection of the *puruṣa* can no longer be identified with the appearance by mistaking it for reality, and, by no longer identifying with it, it overcomes *avidyā* and attains *kaivalya*, supreme Liberation.

> '*Kaivalya* follows the re-absorption of the *guṇas* [or the three constitutive elements], because they are devoid of purpose for the *puruṣa*; [there is *kaivalya*] when the consciousness is founded on its own essence.'[1]

[1] *Ibid.* IV, 34.

The eight means or aṇgas

Rājayoga, therefore, directs the attention to the mind rather than to the body or the emotions. Thus it seeks to control *citta*, the substance of mind, with its products or *vṛttis*, the thought waves which, if uncontrolled, take the *jīva* (the embodied soul) into the sea of *saṁsāra*.

The position of *Rājayoga* is clear: the various *prāṇa*s of the body and the emotions and senses depend on the mind (*manas*). If the mind were not to function, the gross physical realm and that of the subtler senses would be nothing but automata. Perception takes place at the level of mind, sensation is perceived by the mind, and the body itself can be controlled and directed by a mind which has understood its own movement. Just as in the science of physics the control of the process of energy entails control at the molecular level and at the level of external matter, in the same way the control of *citta* and the *vṛttis* means that the entire psycho-sensory and physical process is mastered and thus given direction.

It should be said that within the limits of individuality the mental realm is the highest, that which synthesises all the energy currents of *prāṇa* and the coarse body. It is inevitable, therefore, that it claims great importance, and *Rājayoga*, or Patañjali's *Yogasūtra*, gives it full attention, even though it also makes use of postures (*āsanas*) and *prāṇāyāma*, the pillars of *Haṭhayoga*, placing them, however, under the direction of the mind. *Rāja*, then, is the royal *yoga* because it operates throughout the entire realm of individuality.

Another value that should be assigned to *Rājayoga* is that of entering upon *sādhanā* by purifying the emotions and the mind. On the other hand, without the preliminary cleansing away of undesirable psychic contents, this type of *yoga* could turn out to be very dangerous, not only at the level of *manas* but also at the physical level. According to the classical *darśana*, the act of purification falls into two stages, which correspond to the five *yama*s and the five *niyama*s, the first two of the eight *aṅgas* (means) of *Rājayoga*.[1]

The *yama*s, as we have seen elsewhere, are rules of moral conduct: seek the truth and abstain from doing wrong, stealing, coercion, and so on. They entail mastering the tendencies of *rajas* (*rajoguṇa*) which incite acquisitiveness, the birth of passions, egoism, and so on. The main purpose of these rules is to soothe the thirst of acquisitive extroversion, and therefore of *rajoguṇa*, to empty the mind of its excessively imprisoning contents and its strong opposition to a precise activity of psychosomatic direction.

The *niyama*s also belong to the realm of 'discipline', allowing the energies of the mind to be modelled on the rhythm of *sattva*.

Rājayoga can be undertaken without any fear, if this preliminary discipline has been completed in such a way that it has become a *habitus*. The true withdrawal or abstraction of the consciousness from the senses (*pratyāhāra*) will take place easily if the mind has been purified of particular items of obscuring and conditioning dross. And so, in their turn, concentration (*dhāraṇā*), meditation (*dhyāna*), and *samādhi* can be realised, if

---

[1] See Śaṅkara, *Aparokṣānubhūti*, verses 102-105, edited by Raphael. Aurea Vidyā, New York.

an effective withdrawal of the consciousness from the objects of sense has been made.

The aim of *Rājayoga* is not just to quieten the turbulent thought-modifications or to propound specified rules of ethical conduct. *Rājayoga* goes beyond this, for its true purpose is to slow down the movement of the three *guṇas* to the point where it can bring about their re-absorption into *prakṛti* (primordial substance), thereby leaving the *puruṣa/jīva* in complete freedom. This condition is called *kaivalya*. In the state of *kaivalya* the *puruṣa* is established in its own real nature, which is pure consciousness, free of all translational movement around the objects/events of *prakṛti*. It needs to be remembered, however, that *Rājayoga* is the path of ardent will, the path of the disciple who is afire with 'the will to be'. The will to reach the Divine is such that the strong-willed disciple is able to subdue his own lower urges and lay on the altar of the Godhead a being that is transformed and transfigured. Obstacles do not exist for a will that seeks the Supreme.

What is it that obstructs union? What is it that hinders spiritual progress and 'consummation'? *Rājayoga* answers, 'It is an undisciplined human/animal nature, which chains the neophyte to the world of incompleteness. It is a restless and inconstant mind, which creates separations and distances.' So an individual who desires perfection must focus his efforts on mastering his own lower nature, on transforming and sublimating all his energies so that he can project them, in their purity and transparency, towards the object of his desire. If great devotion, dedication, and surrender to the Godhead are the factors in *Bhaktiyoga* which propel the disciple towards the great union, in *Rājayoga* it is the *will* to be *kaivalya* that produces a dynamic action of constant uplift until the end of the journey is reached.

Rājayoga is for those who wish to master, mould, and direct their own individualised nature. It is also a method of conscious liberation, for all the lower vibrations of the being come to be sublimated. The active will of the *rājayogi* is the higher octave of the desire/feeling of the *bhaktayogi*.

Radhakrishnan says:

> 'By powerfully implementing the will, we are able to suppress the thoughts which make so much noise in our mind, as well as unworthy desires. By means of an active engagement which never ceases, the *yogi* is called to take control.'[1]

Through the path of *Rājayoga* there is the possibility of developing powers/*siddhis* related to the processes of the lower psyche, but the true *yogi* who seeks liberation from incompleteness takes no heed of it and is not distracted, for his is a flight to *kaivalya*.

The will comes forth and shows itself at the mental level, as feeling/devotion does at the emotional level. The strong-willed seeker sets himself at the level of mind, and it is from there that he initiates his great alchemical process of transformation.[2]

The *rājayogi* has a positive attitude with regard to the Godhead, in contrast to the receptive attitude of the *bhaktayogi*. On the pathway of *Rājayoga* it is the individual himself who takes himself by the hand and raises himself to the Divine; so what is needed is a psychological knowledge of oneself: a comprehension of

---

[1] S. Radhakrishnan, *Bhagavadgītā*, 'Introduction', page 73, op. cit.

[2] To go deeper into the alchemical realisative process see 'The Fire of Life. Realisation according to Alchemy', in *The Threefold Pathway of Fire*, by Raphael, where there are parallels with the realisative aspect pertaining to the *Rājayoga*, op. cit.

one's mental processes[1] and a knowledge of the subconscious realm, so that the obstacles can be removed and overcome, and union can be attained.

Rāja means 'royal' and *yoga* means 'union', and so *Rājayoga* is the royal *yoga* for realising union. It is also that which synthesises other types of *yoga*. Its fundamental notes are meditation (*dhyāna*) and contemplation (*samādhi*), and thus it is also known as *Dhyānayoga* or *Samādhiyoga*. It is a compendium of philosophy, psychology, and realisative mysticism. Its points of reference are the *Vedas/Upaniṣads*, and, as we have seen, it proposes eight means (*aṅgas*) or steps that finally lead to *kaivalya*, which consists of the liberation of the Spirit/*puruṣa* from the modifications of *prakṛti* (primordial substance; the 'primordial waters').

Let us review the eight means of *Rājayoga*: *yama* (self-control), *niyama* (observances), *āsana* (postures), *prāṇāyāma* (control of the breath of *prāṇa*), *pratyāhāra* (abstraction), *dhāraṇā* (concentration), *dhyāna* (meditation), *samādhi* (contemplation/*enstasi*).

Let us now examine more closely the last three means: *dhāraṇā*, *dhyāna*, and *samādhi*.

[1] See 'The processes of the mind' in *Self-knowledge*, edited by the Kevala Group. Aurea Vidyā, New York.

Dhāraṇā

Dhāraṇā consists in fixing the mind on a *pratyaya* (content/seed of concentration), by excluding from the mental field all the other possible *pratyayas* which might intrude. It is thus the mind's first act of withdrawing. The importance of this *aṇga* is easy to appreciate if one acknowledges that the mind always tends to be 'scattered', to jump from one item to the next, to be constrained by the necessity of psychic becoming, genuine *saṁsāra*. The being needs to know how to withdraw itself to the centre of its psychosomatic system and from there begin the rectification of the 'inner breakdown'. A mind that is not collected cannot be creative. A restless and scattered mind really belongs to someone who is subject to the world of *māyā/avidyā*.

Mental restlessness is not a cause but an effect resulting from the unceasing stimulation of the subconscious and the over-sensitive, excessively impressionable emotional body. To eliminate these causes of restlessness, it is necessary to practise the first five *aṇgas*, which essentially have this preliminary function.

The inner world of the psyche is a *chaos*, which means that a cosmos needs to be created by taking the soul back, step by step, to its pre-adamitic condition. The first step is to position oneself at the centre of one's own psychosomatic system, and *dhāranā* represents this positioning of consciousness. Concentration is the result of *attention*. Wherever there is attention, there is concentration, by means of which all the 'powers' are focussed on the *pratyaya* under consideration.

Dhyāna

Dhyāna is a prolonged concentration and constitutes the foundation of all the individual's potential creativity. It is the instrument by which the senses are brought under control. *Dhyāna* opens the gates to *samādhi*. It is the royal means that God has given to man for self-attainment. It is the bow by which the disciple/archer hits the target. *Dhyāna* is the highest psychic faculty after intelligence: an intelligence without a harmonised mind is unable to manifest itself. By means of *dhyāna* the psychic powers are consciously and deliberately co-ordinated, integrated, and directed according to a pre-established cause. *Dhyāna* is the instrument which can take us into conflict, error, suffering or into the bliss of *samādhi*.

Dhyāna constitutes a *continuous*, uninterrupted flow (this is how it differs from *dhāraṇā*) of thought-energy centred on the pre-selected *pratyaya*. Our psychic powers, both conscious and subconscious, can find their solution only through a mind that is stable, ready and able to dissolve or coagulate. Every emotional movement – even though it may bring happiness – is but a fleeting and evanescent movement. Unless it is built on the firm foundations of *dhyāna*, which is of the order of the mind, one may reach intermittent states of mystical emotion, because emotion without direction from the mind fluctuates and is incomplete, excessively individual (it follows the law of attraction and repulsion) and is the cause of serious psychic disturbances, in addition to being a factor of mere opinion.

Dhyāna may be focussed on a *pratyaya* that is concrete or abstract, with form or without, and so it encompasses a vast sweep of activities. Meditation may therefore be devoted to a *yantra* (a simple or complex figure or geometrical symbol), a sound – such as a *mantra* – a colour (light), and so on. All these seeds – given according to the disciple's susceptibility – effect appropriate changes in consciousness. The symbol is cathartic and fosters transformation.

With continual and intelligent practice, one can come to meditate for hours without the least mental distraction, even though external stimulations or disturbances may impinge.

A mind that is under control, at peace, and always ready is vigilant; and active vigilance, say the Buddhists, can lead to *nirvāṇa*.

'In the beginning was the Word, and the Word was with God, and the Word was God.'[1] The Word is the word of power, and the word is *sound*. Sound is a vibration which, once it is established in being, produces specific effects. We know from science that sound is both creative and destructive, depending on the use that is made of it. It was on the 'primordial waters' that sound impressed its notes. The human being, too, 'made in the image of the Creator', possesses the creative principle of the Word.

By means of the meditation of sound, *yantra*, and so on, the individual produces certain specific results upon the 'waters' or the psychosomatic substance. Sound is an idea that is caused to vibrate. In deep meditation, when seeds/*bījas* or sounds vibrate, then space, which is

[1] St John, 1:1.

life, responds. *Mantra*s are powers sounding in limitless space; they can be caught and transmitted, and this is what the Vedic *ṛṣis* did.

God (the Word) visualised, and the worlds came forth from the abyss of darkness. At certain levels, sound becomes light (hence there is *dhyāna* on colour), which triumphs over the darkness.

Through *dhāraṇā* the creative mind/instrument is fixed. Through *dhyāna* the Idea/seed/word is uttered. Through *samādhi* the unity of subject/object, or the incarnation of the Word, is realised.

Prayer is the expression of emotion. Meditation is the mind's act of power. *Samādhi* is the work of the *buddhi* (another body of the soul's manifestation).

We can synthesise the meditative process by showing some correlations:

Mantra	Sound	Spirit/*ātman*
Colour	Quality/Light	Soul/*jīvātman*
Yantra	Form or plane	Body/*sthūlaśarīra*

These three notes can be sounded in particular *cakras*, or vital centres, to produce precise effects. They can also be combined with *prāṇāyāma* (prāṇic breathing) and *mudrās* (gestures).

If one bears in mind that the *jīvātman* (soul), a reflection of the *ātman*, dwells in the deepest and most secret cavity of the heart, and that it is covered by many superimpositions of the order of sense-based *manas*, one can understand the enormous importance of these techniques of meditation.

Regaining the pre-adamitic nature is the work of initiation, not of mere mental speculation or simply calling upon the name of the Father with one's lips.

Samādhi

Meditation that is steady and incisive on a *pratyaya* leads consistently to *samādhi*.

These three aspects – *dhāraṇā*, *dhyāna*, and *samādhi* – are nothing but three moments in a single process. In fact, the three taken together are called *saṁyama*. To practise *saṁyama* on a *pratyaya* is to go step by step into *samādhi*.

> 'Grasping the bow, which is the powerful weapon contemplated in the *Upaniṣads*, fix the well-whetted arrow. Pull [the string], with the consciousness absorbed in meditation on That. My beloved, hit that very target which is the Imperishable.
>
> 'The *pranava* is the bow, the *ātmā* is the arrow, and the *Brahman* is said to be its target. It must be pierced by one who is not distracted, who must become one with That, just as the arrow [becomes one with the target].'[1]

Samādhi is characterised by various phases. In its final phase it represents the penetration of the essence of the *pratyaya*, the realisation of the ultimate ipseity of the *pratyaya*, beyond subject and object.

To explain *samādhi* as contemplation is to run the risk of distorting the precise meaning of the Sanskrit term, given that, in the West, contemplation is generally understood as the mere visualisation of a datum.

---

[1] See *Muṇḍaka* Upaniṣad II,II,3-4.

First of all, *samādhi* has no relationship with emotion, imagination, or any individualised psychic power. At the level of *dhyāna*, one is duality and objectivity. In *samādhi*, one has gone beyond empirical and objective duality and finds oneself in *subtle* dimensions. A state of happiness, for example, can be evoked through emotion, can be imagined, thought about, intuited; but such things concern the psychic realm in which subject and object operate. It is one thing to intuit or imagine, and another thing to experience happiness with the whole consciousness. Thus it is one thing to imagine or 'face', and another thing to *be*.

Samādhi connotes the direct experience of truth, without the mediation of *manas* (the empirical reasoning mind); and since there are different degrees of the single truth/reality, there are also different degrees of *samādhi*. *Rājayoga* lists some of these, which we shall mention briefly.

First of all, there are two categories of *samādhi*: with a seed, or *bīja*, and without a seed. They are:

- *saṁprajñāta samādhi*, or *sabīja samādhi*
- *asaṁprajñāta samādhi*, or *nirbīja samādhi*.

Saṁprajñāta Samādhi can be subdivided into:

- *savitarka* and *nirvitarka*
- *savicāra* and *nirvicāra*
- *sānanda* and *nirānanda*
- *sāsmitā* and *nirasmitā*.

To understand these terms it is good to consider that every datum presents two aspects: *rūpa* (objective form) and *svarūpa* (the actual essence of the datum).

In the case of the *manas*/mind which finds itself in the state of *dhyāna*, the *rūpa* is the *pratyaya* of meditation, the formal object; the *svarūpa*, on the other hand, coincides with the subjective nature of the mind itself, abstracted from its ideal content. So the level of *savitarka* and the level of *nirvitarka*, for example, correspond to the objective functional condition and the non-objective functional condition; the functional condition, because these states merely indicate the function of the *citta* (the whole of the psychic content) rather than the levels at which it operates. They concern the function rather than the substantial structure of the level of manifestation.

To have a better grasp of these functions we may, in fact, relate them to the levels or vehicles which the soul uses to express itself at the various levels of experience.

Savitarka is the function of *manas* at the subtle level of *manas*, abstracted from the objective material data. *Savicāra* is the function of the *buddhimayakośa* or the *vijñānamayakośa* (the vehicle made of intellect), abstracted from the conditioning of *manas*. *Sānanda* is the function of the *ānandamayakośa* (the sheath, vehicle, or body for the expression of bliss), abstracted from the support of the *buddhi* or intellect. *Sāsmitā* is the function of the *jīva* in its ipseity, its noumenality, abstracted from all the bodies of manifestation.

At the level of *jīva* or *ātmā*, the purified soul, there exists only the consciousness which abides in itself, lives for itself and with itself. In *sānanda samādhi*, there subsist the being (*svarūpa*) and the object/*bīja* (*rūpa*), represented by *avidyā* (primordial ignorance). In *sāsmitā samādhi*, the being is abstracted from its *rūpa* and is ready to be re-integrated into pure Spirit, into the *ātman*/*Brahman*, or – in the specific case of *Rājayoga* – into the sovereign *puruṣa*. We could express these last two *samādhi*s conceptually as 'I am this' and 'I am', whereas in *asaṁprajñātasamādhi* or *nirbīja samādhi* the 'I am' resolves, according to *Advaita Vedānta*, into *That* or *Turīya*, and, according to *Rājayoga*, into the *puruṣa* isolated from *ahaṁkāra* (the sense of 'I') and from the modifications of *prakṛti*.[1]

[1] To go deeper into the various types of *samādhi* see *Dṛgdṛśyaviveka* (A philosophical investigation into the nature of the 'Seer' and the 'seen'). Translation from the Sanskrit and commentary by Raphael. Aurea Vidyā, New York.

JÑĀNAYOGA

Jñānayoga, or the *yoga* of knowledge, aims above all at 'knowing' the Godhead.

If God is the ultimate truth/reality among all the possible contingent truths, then that which is not Truth is ignorance, blindness, and illusion. So the aim of the *jñāni* is to remove the illusion, the ignorance, and the darkness, and to grasp the Truth and the revealing light. This path requires a mind that is developed and sensitive to the huge questions about Being and Non-Being.

The great aspiration of the *jñāni* is the 'search' for absolute truth, not partial truth, for partial truth is investigated and discovered by the analytical/selective mind (*manas*).

Only when truth has been found does the disciple immerse himself into that which he has always yearned for, with an act of 'unification and incarnation'. The *jñāni* is the one who incarnates and manifests wisdom.

Facing him are three factors that need to be resolved:

- the knowing subject
- knowledge
- the object of knowing.

Slowly these three factors have to merge together and become wholly one. The *jñāni* is able to realise the truth because he himself is truth.

By means of knowing, the object is absorbed into the knowing subject. This is not the way of the scientist, the theologian, or the mere intellectual, as might seem to be the case at first sight, but it is the way of the intuitive/contemplative philosopher (Socrates, Plato, Plotinus, Śaṅkara, and others). It is the way of the metaphysician. It is the way of one who works with the kind of thought which is synthetic, plastic, supra-sensory, and which leads to 'immediate discernment'.

The *jñāna* enquiry consists of silence, intuition, flashes of enlightenment, visions, the discovery of the noumenal, detachment, and dispassion. It is not the way of passive devotion to a Being about which there is no desire to know or learn anything. It is not the way of willing to be, through an intentional act of power. It is not the way of action. But it is the way of 'intuitive discernment'. It is the way which penetrates the ultimate mysteries of reality, the way which works with Ideas and ideal, synthetic, and archetypal Principles. It is a way of solitude and abstractions; it requires time and long periods of contemplation, which, we repeat, is not of the order of the senses and devotion.

It might appear to be the way of the West, but it is not. The Western mind is more analytical, critical, discursive, extrovert. The Westerner is more inclined to activism, more occupied with making material things and finding ways of gratifying the physical body.

The requirements for a way of this kind are, by contrast, a withdrawal into oneself; an active internalisation; a centripetal movement; a mind that can quickly embrace the objective manifestation and the inner life; a capacity for deduction, an 'understanding' of the connections between life and form, between spirit and matter, God and nature, cause and effect; an ability to delve into the world of *meanings*; a great, endless thirst for spiritual truth; a constant, daily attitude of meditation/contemplation. The more the disciple rids himself of that which is not, the more he lives and embodies that which is.

> 'And ye shall know the truth, and the truth shall make you free.'[1]

This is the watchword of the *jñāni*. This is why he devotes all his resources to revealing the Truth and *being* the Truth.

> 'The way of Knowledge aims at the realisation of the one supreme Self. It seeks right discrimination, *viveka*, through the method of intellectual reflection, *vicāra*. It observes and distinguishes the different elements of our apparent and phenomenal being and, by refusing to identify itself with them, it comes to put aside those constituents of *prakṛti*, that is, phenomenal Nature, or the creations of *māyā*, that is, phenomenal consciousness. In this way it reaches identification with the one Self, which is pure, immutable, imperishable, unfathomable by any phenomenon or any combination of phenomena. From this moment, in accordance with habitual practice, one rejects the phenomenal world from the consciousness as an 'appearance' and reaches the final absorption (from which there is no return) of the soul into the Supreme.'[2]

Let us also cite some words of Svāmi Śivānanda, taken from his book *Jñāna Yoga* and interspersed with our own considerations:

> '*Jñāna Yoga* is the "royal way" and is described in all the practical treatises of *Vedānta*. The starting-point lies in a heightened [spiritual] perception of the Vedāntic texts through the mediation of a qualified

---

[1] St John, 8:32.

[2] Sri Aurobindo, *The Synthesis of Yoga*, Introduction to Volume I. Ubaldini, Roma 1967.

teacher. Only the *Upaniṣads* can give precise knowledge of the *Brahman*. Really *hearing* them, from the beginning to the end, can persuade the hearer of the extreme importance of all the sacred texts and show him the identity of the individual soul with the *Brahman*.

'The second step consists in *comprehending* what has been *heard*. Reason has the right to examine the Scriptures from all angles. As far as the nature of the *Brahman* is concerned, reasoning allows all objections to be set aside. Belief in the absolute nature of the Self – acknowledged through hearing and reflecting – is then verified through *experience* by means of meditation upon the Self. Meditation that is constant reveals all the false superimpositions, all the obstacles arising from the impressions left by past actions, thereby revealing the true nature of the Self.'

'The moment one is aware of this absolute *ātman*, the world of appearances and its cause, *māyā*, disappear. The aspirant has then arrived at his destination and becomes a *paramahaṁsa*, a perfect being: "The knot of the heart is cut, all doubts are dispelled, and for him [the effects of all] actions are destroyed, when That, supreme and not supreme, has been realised" (*Muṇḍaka Upaniṣad*, II,II,8).'

'The aim itself can be attained through contemplating the *Brahman*, stripped of all attributes. The sacred texts clearly show that perfect contemplation of the Absolute is another way to liberation: "This cause can be comprehended through reflecting on its nature by means of the Vedāntic texts, as well as by contemplating its absolute nature."

> 'A perfect *jñānayogi* can teach philosophy and meditation to two different disciples from the respective viewpoints of their mental dispositions.'[1]

Hearing, *reflecting*, and *meditating* are the three steps practised by the *jñāni* disciple.[2] Hearing is not to be confused with merely physical perception through the senses; it requires deep attention, born from a mind that is disciplined, humble, and alert. Reflection is not simply analytical (and therefore does not arise only from the head) but is synthetic/intuitive and therefore comes from the heart also. It is a particular way of *understanding.* Meditation is the revelation of reality itself. For a *jñāni*, to meditate is to *be*.

> '*Jñāna* is not intellectual knowledge, not mental understanding, not instinctive recognition, not a mere intellectual feeling. It is the direct realisation of one's own unity with the supreme Being. It is *paravidyā*. Intellectual conviction alone will never be able to lead to *brahmajñāna*.
>
> 'The mind of a *jñāni*, strictly speaking, should not even be given this name; it is pure Reality. Mind is that which moulds the diversity of objects, but the mind of the *jñāni* is like the copper which an alchemical operation has transformed into gold. ... A mind which, though participating in the world of objects, stays detached from it may be considered to be like *Brahman* itself.'[3]

According to the traditional philosophy of *Vedānta*, there are four states of consciousness, as listed below:

---

[1] Svāmi Śivānanda, *Jñāna Yoga*, Chapter LXI, Editions Albin Michel, Paris 1958, verse 529.

[2] See *Bṛhadāraṇyaka Upaniṣad*, II,IV,5, and Śaṅkara, *Vivekacūḍāmaṇi*, *śloka* 70, op. cit.

[3] Svāmi Śivānanda, *Jñāna Yoga*, Chapter LXI, verses 530-534, op. cit.

Microcosm	Macrocosm
Vaiśvānara	*Virāṭ*
Taijasa	*Hiraṇyagarbha* or *Sūtrātma*
Prājña	*Īśvara*

Turīya/The Fourth/*Brahman*

'*Jñānayoga*, or the *Yoga* of Knowledge, is a difficult path. Many people have only an intellectual view of it, but without reaching Realisation.'[1]

The danger of *Yogavedānta*, or *Jñānayoga*, lies in stopping merely at conceptual cognition. When the Truth, revealed by intuitive discernment, does not come to be integrated into the context of the whole being, so as to produce a complete transformation, one falls into a sterile and superficial knowledge which is of no use. It is not enough to know that our bodies are transient, molecular compounds: *it is necessary* to *truly* consider them as such.

Observing the last three methods described above, we may add that the *bhaktayogi* 'overcomes the world' through love of the Godhead; the *rājayogi* overcomes the world because he has been able to master it and transcend it; and the *jñāni* overcomes it because he has *comprehended* it and recognised it as unreal. But, as may be noted, the aim is to transcend all that exists.

'My kingdom is not of this world' ... 'even as I am not of the world.'[2]

---

[1] *Ibid.* verse 538.

[2] St John, 8:36; 17:14.

ASPARŚAYOGA or ASPARŚAVĀDA

'Man does metaphysics as he does breathing, without thinking about it.'[1]

Embedded in human nature is the spontaneous need to transcend itself and to set goals which are always beyond its transient dimension. Metaphysics was born with the cosmos itself, for every particle of the universe reaches out towards its total existential re-integration.

Man is a restless being, always driven to transcend himself or to surmount his own natural condition, to reach another world which is difficult to define but which effectively represents a denial or rejection of all limitation and is thus a denial of the compound finite world of appearances.

'The secret of the method consists in looking carefully into everything for that which is most absolute.'[2]

The need for the Absolute is the primary need in man's mind. It implies that within all the orders of reality there must be a first term (*ādi*) which is the condition for all the rest – and, as such, is independent, at least within its own order – and which, in the strictest sense of the term, may be considered to be absolute and the sole absolute without any second.

---

1 Emile Meyerson, *De l'explication dans les sciences*. Payot, Paris 1927.

2 Descartes, *Regulae ad directionem ingenii*, VI.

It may be noted that the philosophy (especially modern Western philosophy) which questions man's ability to discover the Absolute is merely transferring the character of absoluteness to the world of sensible experience.

The metaphysical philosopher travels along the direct way of complete awareness and cognitive re-integration into absolute Being, the root of all that exists. Rather than being interested in the world, rather than seeing how the 'object/universe' has been made and looking at its laws and its magical phenomena, rather than acquiring a power over form (a *siddhi*), he aims for the a-principial Being, or Non-Being, the undifferentiated, the ineffable, the unknowable (by means of the senses).

Metaphysics is interested in that which is 'beyond physics', beyond nature, beyond the gross, subtle, and causal forms, the substantial, the principial Being, the God-Person, the objective and the subjective, and all possible polarity. This implies that metaphysics deals with the constant, the infinite[1], Non-Being in the sense of pure, single Being, the unconditioned, the One without a second (*advaita*).

If metaphysics is the inquiry into Reality without a second, then it cannot be put into a mould, conceptualised, or made to fit into individual mental frameworks. The Absolute, the supreme Reality, cannot be circumscribed, represented, or brought to the level of an empirical relativism, and it cannot be made the exclusive property of an individual or a nation.

---

[1] See Chapter IV, commentary to *kārikā* 97, Gauḍapāda, *Māṇḍūkyakārikā*, Translated from Sanskrit and edited by Raphael. Aurea Vidyā, New York. 'The Infinite has neither size (big or small) nor duration (succession of moments, long or short); the Infinite is beyond all size and duration because it is neither space nor time, even though these may be extended to the unlimited'.

For metaphysical realisation there are undoubtedly certain prerequisites, and the first of them all is a mind that is able to synthesise and to comprehend the atemporal.

Most individuals are yoked to time, space, and causality, from which it is indeed difficult to escape. But if one wants to realise metaphysical knowledge, one has to *fly*, go beyond time and space, beyond the contingent, the individual and the general. In other words, one has to be able to abide *without supports*. Hence the name *asparśa*, which means 'without contact, relationship, or support'. Hence, also, the proper attention that we must give it, for we are facing a particular and special kind of knowledge which does not operate in a way that is conformable to the discursive or empirical way of knowing that is commonly employed. This constitutes the true 'Way of Fire', because its touch burns away all objectivising possibility of *māyā*, and because the being is revealed and shown in its self-radiance. To catch hold of a-temporality in the instant means non-reliance on any empirical *yogic* practice or psychosomatic exercise; it means suddenly going into the depths of the all-embracing, all-pervading present. Metaphysical realisation can be effected through that specific type of mind that may be called *mens informalis*.[1]

By whom has this metaphysical *yoga* been proposed? By the *Upaniṣads* and by the commentaries of Gauḍapāda and Śaṅkara, the two great Masters of *Advaita Vedānta*.

In his *kārikā* Gauḍapāda declares:

> 'I bow down to that *yoga*, taught by the Scriptures themselves and well known as *asparśa*, free of re-

---

[1] See 'Metaphysical Realisation' in *The Pathway of Non-Duality*, by Raphael, op. cit.

lationship, beneficent, the bestower of bliss for all beings, devoid of all opposition and contradiction.'

Śaṅkara comments:

'*Asparśayoga* is the *yoga* that has no *sparśa*, no contact, no relationship, with anything: its nature is indeed that of the *Brahman*. The knowers of *Brahman* call it by this name; in other words, the *yoga* that is free of all causal relationship is called *Asparśayoga*. It becomes *sarva sattva sukha*: a blessing for all beings. Some aspects of *yoga* – for example, austerity (*tapas*) – are, however, associated with suffering, although they are said to confer intense happiness; but this *yoga* does not belong in this category. What, then, is its nature? It is bliss for all beings. We may say that the enjoyment of a particular kind of object may bring happiness, but not steadfast well-being [enjoyment of any order and degree is always dualistic, and therefore brings conflict]; *Asparśayoga*, by contrast, leads to Bliss and, at the same time, to steadfast well-being, because its nature transcends impermanence. Moreover, it is free of oppositions. Why? Because it is devoid of contradiction. To this *yoga*, taught by the Scriptures, I bow down.'[1]

'This *yoga*, which is named *asparśa* (without any contact) is difficult to comprehend for many aspiring *yogis*, because they, fearing [annihilation] where there is none, are afraid of it.'

Śaṅkara continues:

'*Asparśayoga nāma*: this is known as the *Yoga of asparśa*, without contact/support, because it has no relationship [with anything], and so is in contact with

[1] Gauḍapāda, *Māṇḍūkyakārikā*, IV, 2, Translated from Sanskrit and edited by Raphael, op. cit.

nothing. It is described in the *Upaniṣads*. A *yoga* of this kind is difficult to access for those *yogis* who are deprived of the true knowledge of the *Upaniṣads*. The idea is that this truth can be realised only in consequence of a surge whose fulfilment represents an awareness of the *ātman* as the single reality [without a second]. *Yogina bhayadarśina abhaye asmāt bibhyati*: *yogis* are afraid [of this *yoga*], but they have no need to be afraid. Those without discrimination fear that the practice of this *yoga* will extinguish their individuality, although [*asparśa*] is beyond all fear.'[1]

The designation *Asparśayoga* seems to contain a contradiction, because *asparśa* means 'no contact' and *yoga* means 'contact, union of things'. The first is with reference to that which is without relationship, implying absolute Non-duality, which by its very nature cannot have any contact with things because, from the viewpoint of ultimate truth, there can exist nothing but the Absolute within its unique Infiniteness. The second term, on the other hand, implies the relationship and contact of two data: the creature and the Creator, the individual *jīva* and *Īśvara*, the individual consciousness and the universal consciousness, and so on.

Gauḍapāda gives the name of *yoga* to the way that leads to the Absolute, to the One without a second, to the *nirguṇa Brahman*, with no exceptions, a working means of eliminating the obstacles which prevent truth from showing itself; it may represent Platonic Dialectic.

'The knowledge of the enlightened being, the knowledge that is all-pervading, has no relationship with any object; in the same way, too, souls have no relationships with objects.'[2]

---

[1] Gauḍapāda, *Māṇḍūkyakārikā*, III, 39, op. cit.

[2] *Ibid* IV, 99.

Here the emphasis is on the fact that knowledge (*Brahman*) which is all-pervading and homogeneous, like space/ether, has no relationship with objects, which are nothing but mere appearances. The *Brahman* is unborn, free of differences, without a second. *Asparśavāda* thus embarks upon the road which leads directly to the realisation of the absolute, transcendent Being. Its viewpoint is of a pure metaphysical order, because its flight is directed to the non-dual principle, without descending to the slightest degree of duality. It constitutes the authentic 'Philosophy of being', Being pure and single, the One-Good of Plato, the Being of Parmenides, and the One of Plotinus.

The difficulty of grasping absoluteness is considerable, because it is not with the mind – which operates in the realm of subject and object – that absolute Non-duality can be comprehended. Vain are the efforts of those who tend to posit the Absolute as a mere object of mental representation. We may say that this *yoga*, to be truly comprehended, necessarily and univocally demands an approach of identity. In other words, since it is a *yoga* without relationships, it is, of course and above all, a *yoga* without supports. Thus one is required to put oneself immediately into the metaphysical Foundation of all that exists, and while all that exists cannot exist without *That*, *That* has its *raison d'être* even without all that exists.

The other types of *yoga* necessarily require a vertical leap, an impulse which always starts from individuality as an effect and is directed to its own transcendence; they therefore require an aspiration towards something. On the path of pure metaphysics there is no longer a question of an aspiration but the actual awareness of being. The disciple is not urged on, but restrained; we may say that he is obliged, not to acquire something higher or lower, but to resolve every instance of *māyā*, including that of union as generally understood.

The disciple of *Asparśavāda* internalises himself and *comprehends* the Absolute, which displays itself in all its majesty in the secret cavity of its own heart. Beyond every idea, concept, ideal, idol, and phenomenon, there is *That*, which is the totality, not subject to, or dependent on, any concept or change. The 're-integrated metaphysician' has the power and the privilege of seeing all the phenomena of life in the light of the metaphysical Zero.

Asparśayoga leads to liberation, or rather to active re-integration (liberation cannot truly be spoken of in this kind of *yoga*), and it realises that essence which is one, undifferentiated, and uncreated, or that state which is a-causal, unmanifest, and impersonal, from which every universe/object appears like a chain of luminous perceptions of *māyā*.

Being *is*, and nothing can be added to it. To say that it is 'this or that' indicates that that Being *is not*. Again, to maintain that it can be different from what it is means stating that a datum *is* and simultaneously *is not*. Moreover, if Being has 'become' this or that, it must have come from a Being or from a non-being. If it comes from a non-being, this is an absurd statement, because nothing comes from nothing; if, on the other hand, it comes from Being, then it must be admitted that Being is born from Being, which means that it remains identical to itself in its indivisibility and, in that case, it cannot be said to 'become' or 'be born' or be in another condition, because Being which remains identical to itself undergoes no movement, no birth, no change. Hence the term *ajātivāda* (non-birth).

One needs a certain type of understanding, not of a sensory order, to appreciate that that which is universal and a-formal cannot be transposed into a specific dialectical perspective or into a dogmatic rational conceptuality.

The metaphysical pathway is positioned on the plane of informal intelligence, from which the emotional realm is totally excluded.

This is the type of *yoga* which has pure intuition of things or appearances. It transcends all phenomenology, all common reason, every kind of religion, subjective social morality, and all sensory experiences, for all these result from something mediated and knowable.

On the other hand, to meditate on something which does not correspond to a sensory/formal datum is not easy. The sense-based mind needs to conceive reality in relation to a form, an image, or a concept, and most of the time the image itself imprisons the thinker, who should, on the contrary, always be independent. The metaphysical path presents difficulties, because one has to abandon the normal thinking process and adjust to unaccustomed conditions of comprehending the a-dimensional and the a-formal.

A premature approach to this path could paralyse the normal process of perception and sense-based thought and prevent access to, or the possibility of, a higher comprehension. From this would come mental inertia and endless confusion, with changed states of consciousness, leading to the annihilation of the dynamics of the mind based on representation. This danger can become acute here in the West, because there is a greater propensity for a formal kind of mind to which is attributed, among other things, a unique and irreplaceable value.

This metaphysics is undoubtedly a path which comprehends the Infinite, the Whole, as the Foundation of all that exists, but this *comprehension* is total realisation inasmuch as there is established within the adept an identity which is effective and conscious, not theoretical

– for if this were the case, then the knowledge would be merely of an order that is sense-based or rational/formal – and not potential, for this condition has always existed and never failed.

It is useful to repeat that *Asparśavāda* is not reached through self-imposed discipline, through faith or devotion, or through any action motivated by individual/sensory expression, but through deep, inner self-awareness. Every extrovert movement of energy tends to exhaust itself, for *spirit* is totally free. Once the undivided point is reached, the notion of translational movement disappears. When form is transcended or the reflection is extinguished, the *puruṣa* returns to its essence, which is without cause, time, or space.

Asparśavāda represents the final step and the goal of all experience and all human possibility of expression. Beyond all experience, there is the 'moment' of the total comprehension of our very essence; this is the fulfilment of perfect equilibrium and conditionless pre-existence. The normal individual is fettered to the concepts of causality, time, and space, and therefore to movement, to the evolving object. Few are they who can reveal that *eternal present*, the Alpha and Omega of what is commonly called change. The metaphysician – not content with having known and transcended the limited subject/object – dares to climb up to the a-formal, topmost step of the universal vibrational ladder to ... discover himself.

Asparśavāda may be considered to be the highest expression of spiritual knowledge, that knowledge, or rather that 'comprehension', for self-existent union which leads in all respects from the unreal to the real, from death to life, from the finite to the infinite, from the relative (human/divine) to the unqualified Absolute without a second, from conflictual differentiation to supreme Identity.[1]

[1] See '*Ajātivāda* and *Asparśavāda*', in *The Pathway of Non-Duality*, by Raphael. See also Parmenides, *On the Order of Nature*, edited by Raphael. Aurea Vidya, New York.

REALISATION AND PSYCHOLOGICAL COMFORT

Many are they who approach *yoga*, initiatory organisations and schools, spirituality in general, realisation or liberation, but careful observation shows that there is a little confusion among these seekers.

Those who dedicate themselves to spiritual inquiry should ask themselves first of all what they are really seeking or desiring, then what *yoga* or realisation means to them, and finally what kind of group, organisation, teachers, and so on may be right for their own psychological position and level of consciousness.

We shall now examine – among so many – some *opinions*, which shall, of course, be taken for what they are: mere opinions.

Some think that realisation must entail a greater expansion of the 'empirical ego'. They have been heard to say that some specific character has realised himself because he has satisfied most of his egoic demands. Thus an individual that is well known in the world of economics, politics, art, or culture, and so on, is considered to be realised. In other words, in this case, the meaning and value of realisation have been completely turned on their heads.

Others believe that merely attending or belonging to a church, an esoteric group, a *yoga* group, and so on, means having the right to sit at the 'banquet table of the gods', in contrast to the rest of humanity.

Yet others hold that slavishly and fanatically following a group, a Master, or a *guru* means being already on the 'other shore' or having leapt across the 'abyss'.

Then there are the self-taught who cannot bear to have a guide or an instructor, so that they drown in books and become erudite, under the delusion that they are already initiates or even Masters who are able to guide consciousnesses who are on the way of awakening.

These categories of people (and others as well), are obviously, we might say, tuned to the 'profane' and have little or no yearning for the 'Sacred', because they clearly display the fundamental error in which they are floundering.

There is also a category of aspirants who are on a spiritual quest and have true and honest aspirations, but are also prey to the energies of *rajas* at various levels. These people are scattered, going here and there to satisfy their mental requirements, moving from one *guru* to another, and travelling with the thought that truth, realisation, or liberation is found outside themselves. Yet they do so in good faith.

There are those who attend a group for years but remain passive, without moving, as it were, into a discipleship that is active, self-aware, and well directed, so that the whole group is obliged to drag along behind, like weights. Others, again, although well intentioned, are limited by quite a heavy *karma* which makes them stressed and listless.

Some are too emotional in their behaviour and approach, with all the consequences that this dual energy entails.

There are some neophytes who are decidedly seeking a Master, but only to have him say what they wish to hear, and when this fails to happen they may even react. Of course, the ego always wants gratification and approval, as we shall see later. Others come to blackmail: they practise *yoga* or some discipline or they pursue spirituality on the condition that they find health, economic or professional prosperity, a good marriage (if they are looking for a family), the settlement of family conflicts, and so on; and this is all with conscious and unconscious motivations.

Of course, we shall not speak of those who know perfectly well what they want, where to look and who to look for; such need neither stimuli nor many words, for they are already prepared and well directed.

But let us ask ourselves some questions. What does realisation mean? Who has to be realised? What does liberation mean, and from what do we have to be liberated? What does it mean to be an Initiate?

There are many nowadays who practise *yoga*, for example, but we might ask, What does it mean to practise *yoga*? What does *yoga* require of us? And how many types of *yoga* are there?

A good aspirant, seeker, or would-be initiate (whatever name we use) should gather information and have at least an overview of the various spiritual currents to avoid disappointment later in wasting precious energy, and he should begin to have a hint of a right relationship with realisation.

To answer these questions, we shall have to begin by indicating first of all the nature of the constitution of the being or the person in its totality, according to the view of *yoga*, which is both initiatory and religious, for otherwise certain concepts will always be vague and imprecise. This applies more to the purely Western type or one of 'Western consciousness', who is unable to have a clear view of words, concepts, and occurrences that are outside his cultural *milieu*. The West has been long imbued with the Christian teaching of conciliarism, whose values are specifically religious and whose doctrines concern the God-Person or Father, grace, faith, sin, repentance, obedience, the sacraments, the duality of Creator/creature, the devil, hell, salvation, and so on. These are key concepts from which not even atheists or materialists are free, however strongly they may think they are.

Concepts such as those of realisation and liberation are beyond the Western spiritual vision, and most people cannot avoid approaching them in the context of religion.

Again, some Eastern Masters speak even of knowledge as a means of liberation, but this view is also alien to Western religion, because for the Catholic Christian the means of salvation are faith, good works, and Grace.

We wanted to give some indication, even if slight, to show that people frequently approach things whose implications they do not fully appreciate.

Now, returning to the subject mentioned earlier, we can assert that all the Traditions of the East and the initiatory West postulate that the being is a synthesis of Spirit, Soul, and Body (to use religious terms, as St Paul does); of *noûs*, *psyché*, and *sôma* (according to the Tradition of ancient Greece); of *ātman*, *jīvātman*, and *ahaṁkāra* (in the terms of *Vedānta*); and we could list others, but we shall keep to these same principles, changing only the names.

The *noûs* or *ātman* is the divine spark within us, and is of the nature of the supreme Being. The *psyché* or *jīvātman* is the soul or the mediator between the pure Spirit and *sôma*, between the universal and the individual. Lastly, *ahaṁkāra* represents the objective part of the being, the ego/body/*sôma*, 'like an actor who changes his costume every moment'.[1] Although

---

[1] *Maitry Upaniṣad*, IV,2.

these principles or states of consciousness may express themselves at all levels of existence, they nevertheless have a point of reference, if we are allowed to say so, in space, and they exert their respective influences on particular realms of life.

At this point we must also mention – in accordance with the single universal initiatory Tradition (for fundamentally there is only one Tradition with different branches adapted to the requirements of different people) – those realms of existence in which the life of the being develops. We shall consider the vision of *Vedānta*.[1]

The *ātman* is outside time, space, and causality. It is the pure metaphysical 'state' of the being. The *jīvātman* operates principally on two planes of existence: *brahmaloka* and *hiraṇyaloka*. *Ahaṁkāra* (the principle of individualisation) operates at the levels of *manavaloka*, *kāmaloka*, and *pṛthivīloka*.

Brahmaloka (*loka* = place, state, abode) is the abode of *Brahmā*, Being/Person, the God of the entire manifestation. *Hiraṇyaloka* is, let us say, the place or state of consciousness of the gods, the intelligible world. *Manavaloka* corresponds to the 'third heaven' of which St Paul speaks; it is characterised by the thought process, insofar as we are still in an individualised state, even if it is the highest state accessible to individualisation. *Kāmaloka* is the place or state of consciousness for unsatisfied desires and passions. *Pṛthivīloka* is the realm of the earth, the gross physical plane that we know through the five senses, whereas the other planes are hyperphysical or, as they are called, subtle.

According to the qualities (*guṇas*) which the being expresses, it moves in the direction of one or another

---

[1] Correlations with other traditional branches can be found in books published by Aurea Vidyā, such as *Orphism*, *Platonism*, *Qabbālāh*, and *Alchemy*.

of these realms, so that it will follow the way of *devayāṇa* or the way of *pitṛyāṇa*.

All of this can be shown in the following diagram:

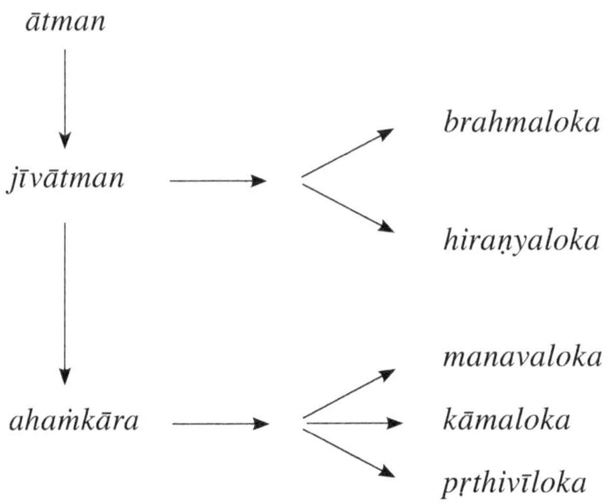

Manas and *kāma* can be synthesised, because wherever one of them is, so is the other one; in fact, we speak of *kāma/manas* to express the mental/sensory state.

When the matter is put like this, in order to understand what is implied by realisation/liberation and what is required of us, we shall have to understand, at this point, something else that is very important and is the foundation and indeed the goal of the realisative process.

If we speak of realisation or liberation, it means that something within us is not realised, is unfulfilled, or is in bondage. We shall therefore have to understand what it is within us that is in bondage or in a state of non-fulfilment.

Let us say at once that the *jīvātman*/soul/*psyché* is merely a reflection of consciousness of the a-temporal *ātman*, a ray of the central sun spoken of by the *Upaniṣads* (*Maitry Upaniṣad*, VI, 26 and 31), and *ahaṁkāra* is, in turn, a reflection of the *jīvātman*. *Ahaṁkāra*, a reflection of a reflection, has 'sundered' itself, weakened its contact with its universal counterpart, so that it has become particularised, individualised, believing itself to be absolute when it is, in fact, as we have seen, nothing but the reflection of a reflection.

To be more precise, we should say that *ahaṁkāra*, as such, is merely the 'sense of I', 'that which begets the ego', a point of reference. It is when it identifies itself with one of its bodies/vehicles and with the qualities of the body that it expresses itself as 'I am this and not something else'. *Asmitā* (I am) is, according to Patañjali's *Rājayoga*, the identification or merging of consciousness with the power of the cognition or quality of the vehicles/bodies of manifestation.

When this happens, there is an 'I am this' in opposition to another 'I am this', with the resulting forgetfulness of one's divine counterpart. In this context a scissure has occurred and the umbilical cord has been so 'slackened' that a separate individuality has been established. With individualisation we therefore have the victory of 'I am I' and 'you are you': I am this body, and you are that body which is different from mine; I have my thoughts and you have yours. In other words, a relative, or rather an appearance, has been made absolute.

Religions speak of a 'fall'. The Christian religion itself tells us that we are fallen angels. By eating the fruit of the Tree of good and evil, Adam fell into the duality of I/you. Plato speaks of the 'fall' of the soul into generation, so that it needs to have its wings restored and be made to fly towards the intelligible world, which is its true homeland.[1]

---

[1] See 'The fall of the Soul', in *The Pathway of Non-Duality*, by Raphael, op. cit.

'My kingdom is not of this world ... just as I am not of the world.'[1] *Vedānta* says that *ahaṁkāra*, a reflection of the *jīva*/soul, has become completely identified, as we have already seen, with its vehicles/bodies of expression and hence with the individualised qualities, forgetting its universal/intelligible origin.

We could continue to give parallels from other Traditions, but, as we have already said, only the names or the concept would change, while the substance would remain the same. Of course, we are speaking of pure initiatory Traditions.

We believe that the reader who has followed us so far will have understood by now what liberation or realisation means. Realisation involves healing a scissure. Liberation involves freeing oneself from all the superimpositions which we have placed over our fundamental reality. *Yoga* – and we are speaking of any kind of *yoga* – means *union*, conjunction. So what has been separated needs to be united; two poles which have been 'loosened' need to be conjoined.

We are of the very *essence* of the supreme Being inasmuch as it *is* and does not become, but by an act of free choice we have identified ourselves with becoming and have forgotten our divine nature. This is the myth of Narcissus, who, being enamoured of his 'shadow' or 'reflection' shown in the water, falls and 'dies' to his previous state of consciousness. However, there is no one to prevent us from resuming our original condition. And the difficulties are represented only by the *degree of identification* that we have effected with our 'shadow', with something that appears and disappears, the changing world of phenomena, which *Vedānta* would call *māyā*.

---

1 St John, 18:36; 17:14.

It is clear that returning to one's original state involves going back into oneself until one discovers oneself to be consciousness without a second, that is, outside of all identification with objects (an instinct, an emotion, a thought are simply 'objects' which can be observed, manipulated, overcome, and transcended).

According to Plato, one has to *remember oneself* as what one really is. The soul that has fallen into self-forgetfulness must re-awaken, according to the beautiful image that Plato has given of the charioteer with two horses, one white and the other black, which are also alchemical symbols.

Let us remind ourselves that we are beings or, rather, *universal consciousness* that is all-inclusive and all-pervading, and we shall have to resume our nature by resolving that second, artificial, and illusory nature which we have created (the nature of the 'shadow') and which has caused us to ignore our divine origin. Such is the identification with this second nature that for most it is difficult, almost impossible, to glimpse the first. Without beating about the bush, we would say that most people are alienated, and it cannot be otherwise.

All who approach any kind of *yoga*, initiatory School, realisative Philosophy, and so on, without knowing these things and without aspiring to close the scissure are either in good faith or they are deceivers.

A genuine Initiate is one who has been able to close the scissure, resolve the 'fall', and transcend that second nature until he rediscovers himself as *unity*. An Initiate is one who has been able to extract the gold from the cave (to use the alchemical expression) and make it shine once more with its own lustre.

Individualisation shows itself in self-assertiveness, as the separate ego, with all the qualifications inherent in the ego. An Initiate worthy of the name, one who is liberated or realised, no longer has anything to do with all this. We may say – and we believe that this will not arouse a 'scandal' or amazement in the Western aspirant – that *there is nothing human* about him (in the sense of *kāma/manas*) because he is something more, or rather, at certain levels, he is the pure *ātman*, outside time, space, and causality. He is one without a second, having integrated all dualities or polarities.

One who is genuinely realised is a 'lamp unto himself'[1], as the *ātman*. He has no need of anything, having extinguished all those desires which belong to the 'shadow'. He lives by his 'own motion'. He is a sun which rotates by itself, spreading 'light' and 'heat'. A desire, whatever its nature and degree, is something unfulfilled, a lack, a deprivation, and these things belong to that 'shadow', because, in fact, *it is not*.

In the title of this chapter we have written 'psychological comfort'. Why? Because – and we must be bold enough to say so – very many people seek only psychological comfort, a way of passing the time, a reason for being with others who are doing something out of the ordinary, a way of resolving conflicts and tensions that have built up in the family, at work, and so on. Or rather, there are *gurus* from both East and West who support these choices, simply aiding the perpetuation of separate individuality so that it is expressed, if necessary, with less tension. Other *gurus* even assist the development of latent psychic powers in order to satisfy vanity and compensate for the psychological frustrations of the student. In short, all these things operate in the realm of psychic individuality in order to maintain and perpetuate that *psychological* empirical *ego* which cor-

---

[1] See *Mahāparinibbānasutta* (the great account of total extinction) in the Pāli Canon.

responds to the plane of the sensible, and not in order to transcend it and resolve it into the ontological I.[1]

On the other hand, in all ages, and therefore not just at the present time, individualisation – the 'scissure' – of necessity has brought, continues to bring, and will always bring conflict, suffering, and alienation; and there is no system of politics, economics, erudition, or empirical science that can provide fulfilment, peace, serenity, and bliss to a consciousness that is alienated and fragmented. Individuality, or the result of the 'fall', is therefore synonymous with pain/suffering (see the four noble truths, which are the foundations of Buddhism), so that, rather than trying to resolve and transcend itself, it seeks only entertainments for its insufficiency, deprivation, and lack of fulfilment.

In fact, on the realisative journey, when one has in view the transcendence of the ego, together with its products, and seeks to effect realisation practically and positively, one notes that individuality flees, withdraws. As long as that individuality, that nature which is second and illusory, merely listens to talks, words, and so on, or is simply satisfied with reading, with *yoga* postures, or with chanting, it welcomes, finds gratification and comfort; but when the consciousness is obliged to go back into itself through suitable processes or techniques, this is the moment of refusal.

Most people are not looking for 'initiatory death', but, paradoxically, they are looking for a way out of conflict while yet remaining in conflict. Most people are looking for psychological compensations in order to be able to 'scrape along' and perpetuate their own 'I am this' until this embodiment expires. Most people are

---

[1] See 'Shadows cast on gurus and on traditional culturalists' in *The Philosophy of Being*, by Raphael. Aurea Vidyā, New York.

looking outside for something that is inside, according to the indications given by all great Initiates, including Jesus. Most people want to be free from troubles while continuing to promote the causes which produce these troubles. In short, most people want to be comforted.

Individuality is eager for comfort and for being accepted, wanted, satisfied, and gratified precisely because it *is not;* and not being an absolute reality, it can never be happy and fulfilled, however much it may be given. So it moves from one desire to another, from one impulse to another, from one event to another (in the world of becoming), without finding a moment's relief or respite.

It frequently happens that most people yield, resign themselves, and devise all sorts of sophistries to convince themselves and others that this is how life is, this is how the world is, and it has to be accepted for what it is. This is a reductive and masochistic view, one that refuses to resolve the problem of one's own incompleteness. And the world is necessarily full of conflicts, suffering, cruelty, and aberrations of all sorts, because that is how we want it; because we make no effort to change its philosophy or the philosophy of our way of living; because we are unwilling to die to a part of us which lives on illusory projections; because we content ourselves with crumbs of consolation which do not solve the problem but, rather, complicate and defer it.

If we take the word 'spirituality' in its widest connotation, we find that it is frequently used as a source of comfort and compensation for those consciousnesses which are unwilling to confront the 'monster' that dwells within them. Even a 'work of charity' may constitute an innocuous source of psychological compensation and comfort. A disciple's action may be twofold; it may always have a compensatory component.

As was indicated earlier, many are weighed down by a heavy *karma*, by psychic disharmony and disturbances, so that they go desperately in search of help or comfort, and if they fail to obtain it, they rebel. In our times, there has also been a reduction in family 'warmth', the feeling of friendship, and even in rest and physical relaxation, because everyone is chasing after material gain in order to meet the requirements of alienating consumerism. But this chase not only fails to lead to Being, but also goes so far as to dehumanise and brutalise, causing greater alienation and creating conflicts of all kinds and, paradoxically, even greater uncertainty.

Others enrol in initiatory Schools for the sake of prestige, or eagerness for titles, responsibility, degrees, and offices, which is to say, as always, for the sake of psychological compensation. And to all these seekers of 'worldly values', to these misfits, who have given up, some *gurus* offer comfort, and someone also offers a kind of purely hedonistic community/society of the *carpe diem* variety, tolerating a quiet licentiousness that goes as far as libertinage, in order to cause the natural deprivation of individuality to be dulled and forgotten. In other words, the biblical 'golden calf' is on offer.

We would say, with all sincerity, that the majority of the Hindu and Buddhist methods of *yoga* that are available in the West offer only therapeutic reasons, so that both the Christian and the profane people are in a good position to classify them as methods that are offered to the ego for its gratification, well-being, and expansion.

The fact is that for realisation, liberation, or true Initiation, precise qualifications are required; in other words, one *has to be ready*. Without a specific *vocation*, a deep *call* from the consciousness (not from the 'beggarly ego'), an ardour for the things which *are* and do not become, one cannot speak of *yoga*, realisation, liberation, or even salvation in the Christian sense. Unless there is a precise prompting for the supra-sensible, it would be better not to embark on the realisative or initiatory process, in order to avoid certain disappointment, which would undoubtedly be a source of further conflicts, and a desecration of that modicum of Sacredness which is desperately trying to resist this *kaliyuga*.

Realisation, as such, bears its own fruit, which is – according to unanimous indications given by two great authentic Teachers (Plato and Śaṅkara) – steadfast Bliss and steadfast Knowledge. Many, however, prefer the conflict that comes from the fickle and contingent nature of sense-enjoyment, the frailty of the gross sensible world, and the pedantry that is based on quantity.

Genuine resolutive knowledge is directed to all. No one is privileged or predestined, even if some are unwilling to accept it and *live* it, with the result that it has to be limited to those few (compared to millions that are 'asleep') who, having been bitten by the snake of harsh *avidyā*, have to some extent awoken to the awareness that something within them is not functioning.

The wish that may be expressed is that all may find Bliss by following the path which is best suited to each one's needs (whether Eastern or Western is of little importance; what is important is that the Way be genuine and pure), because each one, without exception, has within him an inestimable treasure which – through an act of *identification* with the transient and perishable – has been completely forgotten.

The wish is that all may restore wings to the soul, which has fallen into relativity, that it may fly to the supreme heights of objectless Bliss, which is our real nature and which, however 'darkened' or covered it may be, can never be destroyed.

GLOSSARY

abhiniveśa: tendency, attachment, thirst for existence

ādi: the first, the beginning

advaita: Non-duality, One-without-a-second

ahaṁkāra: 'sense of I'

ajātivāda: the doctrine of non-generation expounded by Gauḍapāda in his *Māṇḍūkyakārikā*

ākāśa: 'space', universal ether

ānanda: bliss

ānandamayakośa: sheath of bliss

aṅga: means, operative element

antara: inner

apara: not supreme, lower

aparabhakti: non-supreme *bhakti*

āsana: postures

Asmitā: sense of 'I am', sense of individuality

asparśa: without contact; without relationship or support

asparśavāda: the way of no support

asparśayoga: *yoga* of that which is without contact or relationship

aśvattha: the Tree of life

ātmā: this term indicates the *jīvātman*; the reflection of the *ātman* in the *buddhi*; the *jīva*

ātman: the Self, pure Consciousness, the Absolute within us

avatāra: incarnation of a divine Principle

avidyā: non-knowledge, metaphysical ignorance

bāhya: outer

Bhagavadgītā: 'The Celestial Song'; a poetical and philosophical work in which a realisative and initiatory dialogue unfolds between Kṛṣṇa and Arjuna

bhakta: one who follows the path of devotion

bhakti: devotion, love for the Divine

Bhaktiyoga: the *yoga* of devotion

bīja: seed, content of consciousness

Brahmā: one of the three aspects of the Hindu *Trimūrti*

brahmajñāna: the knowledge of *Brahman*

brahmaloka: the world of *Brahmā*

Brahman or Brahma: the Absolute, absolute Reality
- *nirguṇa*: unqualified, without attributes
- *saguṇa*: qualified with attributes

buddhi: higher intellect, intuition

buddhimayakośa or *vijñānamayakośa*: the sheath of the intellect

cakra: vital energetic centre
- *ājñā*
- *anāhata*
- *mūlādhāra*
- *sahasrāra*

citta: substance of mind

cittavṛtti: modifications of the mind

cittavṛttinirodha: the 'suspension of the modifications of the mind'

darśana: view, 'prospect', in relation to the *Vedas*/*Upaniṣads*, the six orthodox schools of Hindu philosophy

devayāṇa: the Way of the gods

dhāraṇā: concentration

dharma: uprightness; ethical, spiritual duty inherent in the stage of life (*āśrama*). One of the four goals of existence (*puruṣārtha*). In the context of the *Māṇḍūkyakārikā* it is the being, the individualised being

dhyāna: meditation

Dhyānayoga: another name for *Rājayoga*

Gauḍapāda: Śaṅkara's spiritual Teacher, author of the *Māṇḍūkyakārikā*

gītā: song

guṇa: quality, characteristic, the three attributes of *prakṛti* (*sattva*, *rajas*, and *tamas*)

guru: Instructor, spiritual Teacher

Haṭha: constriction, self-coercion, force

Haṭhayoga: the *yoga* of the harmonisation and mastery of the body

Hiraṇyagarbha: the subtle plane of the universal manifestation

hiraṇyaloka: the subtle plane of existence in the universal order

iḍā: one of the three principal *nāḍīs*

Īśvara: qualified Being, the God-Person; designs the causal plane in the universal order as the seed of the gross and subtle manifestations

Īśvarapraṇidhāna: surrender to *Īśvara*,

jīva: living being, individualised soul

jīvātman: the *ātman* which reflects itself in the *jīva*

Jñāna: knowledge, Knowledge/Realisation

Jñānayoga: the *yoga* of Knowledge

jñāni (or *jñānayogi*): one who practises *jñānayoga*

kaivalya: the state of absolute unity (Non-duality)

kaliyuga: the dark age, or the age of iron

kāma: desire, yearning, greed

kāmaloka: the plane of attraction/repulsion

kāma-manas: the relationship between desire and the empirical mind

kārikā: verse, verse commentary; succinct poetical exposition of a philosophical teaching

karma: action, activity, rite, fruit of action

Karmayoga: the *yoga* of 'actionless action'

karmayogi: one who practises *Karmayoga*

karmendriya: organs of action

kleśa: affliction

kośa: sheath, vehicle, energy covering

Kṛṣṇa: in the *Bhagavadgītā* he is the charioteer of Arjuna, to whom he imparts the fundamental teaching concerning 'right action'

kumbhaka: retention of the breath

kuṇḍalini: energy located in the *cakra* at the base of the spinal column

manas: the individualised empirical mind

manavaloka: the world of human beings

mantra: words or sounds of power, hymns used in the rites

Mantrayoga: the *yoga* based on the sacred verbal formulas

māyā: metaphysical ignorance, the phenomenal empirical world. See *avidyā*

mudra: gesture, symbol

nāḍī: 'nerve channel'

nirvāṇa: extinction, solution

niyama: observances; the second *aṅga* of Patañjali's *Rājayoga*

pāda: part, measure

para: higher, supreme

parabhakti: supreme devotion

paramahaṁsa: a realised sage, perfect being

Parapuruṣa: the supreme *puruṣa*

paravairāgya: supreme detachment

paravidyā: supreme Knowledge

Patañjali: codifier of *darśana Yoga*

piṅgalā: one of the three principal *nāḍīs*

pitṛyāṇa: the Way of the Ancestors

Prājña: the state of deep sleep

prajñāta: the content of knowledge

prakṛti: 'nature', primordial substance

prāṇa: vital breath, vital force

praṇava: the sacred syllable Om

prāṇāyāma: prāṇic breathing, control of the breath

pratyāhāra: abstraction, withdrawal of consciousness from the senses, the fifth *aṅga* of Patañjali's *Rājayoga*

pratyaya: content/seed of meditation

prema: unitive love

Premayoga: the *yoga* of love

pṛthivīloka: the realm of the earth, the physical plane

pūraka: inhalation

puruṣa: person, being, universal Man, the 'positive' principle of *Sāṁkhya*

Rāja: royal

rajas: one of the three *guṇas*; corresponds to activity

Rājayoga: the royal *yoga* codified by Patañjali

Rājayogi: one who practises *Rājayoga*

rajoguṇa: the *guṇa* of *rajas*

recaka: exhalation

ṛṣi: sage; one who has realised Knowledge

rūpa: quality, colour, objective form

śabdabrahman: the sound of the *Brahman*, the fundamental note

sādhaka: disciple

sādhanā: spiritual discipline, ascesis

śakti: universal dynamic energy, the energy of the manifestation

samādhi: contemplative identity, direct knowledge of truth

saṁprajñāta: having a content of knowledge
- *asaṁprajñāta*: having no content of knowledge
- *sabīja*: having a seed
- *nirbīja*: not having a seed

Samādhiyoga: another name for *Rājayoga*

Sāṁkhya: one of the six orthodox *darśanas*, codified by Kapila

saṁsāra: cycle of transmigratory becoming

saṁskāra: predisposition, tendency, causal seed

saṁyama: concentration, the assemblage of *dhāraṇā*, *dhyāna*, and *samādhi*

Śaṅkara: codifier of *Advaita Vedānta*, the teaching of Non-duality

sattva: one of the three *guṇas*; corresponds to equilibrium, harmony

siddhi: psychic powers

Śiva: one of the three aspects of the Hindu *Trimūrti*

sthūlaśarīra: the gross body

sūtra: aphorism, verse

sūtrātman: the continuity of consciousness in the *ātman*; sometimes designates *Hiraṇyagarbha*

svarūpa: one's own essential nature

Taijasa: the dream state

tamas: one of the three *guṇas*; it corresponds to inertia, passivity

tantra: doctrinal text, doctrine, treatise

Tantrayoga: the *yoga* of direct experience through the awakening of *kuṇḍalini*

tapas: austerity

Turīya: the 'Fourth', the Absolute, *Brahman*, non-Being

Upaniṣad: 'esoteric teachings', the final part of the *Vedas*

vairāgya: detachment, renunciation

Vaiśvānara: the first 'state' of Being, the waking condition

vāsanā: subconscious mental 'impressions'

Veda: sacred Texts, exposition of sacred traditional Science

Vedānta: the fulfilment of the *Vedas*, one of the six orthodox *darśanas*

Vedānta Advaita: non-dualistic *Vedānta*, codified by *Śrī* Śankarācarya

vicāra: discernment, discriminating inquiry

vidyā: knowledge of Reality, meditation

Virāṭ: the subtle plane of the gross manifestation

viveka: discrimination, intuitive discernment

vṛtti: mental modification, vibration

yama: self-control; the first *aṅga* of Patañjali's *Rājayoga*

yantra: symbolic figure, support

yoga: union, reintegration, one of the six orthodox *darśanas*

Yogasūtra (or *Yogadarśana*): the principal treatise on *yoga*, codified by Patañjali

Yogavedānta: another term for *Jñānayoga*

yogi: one who practises *yoga*

RAPHAEL

Unity of Tradition

Raphael, having attained a synthesis of Knowledge (which is not associated with eclecticism or with syncretism), aims at 'presenting' the Universal Tradition in its many Eastern and Western expressions. He has spent a substantial number of years writing and publishing books on spiritual experience; his works include commentaries on the *Qabbālāh*, Hermeticism, and Alchemy. He has also commented on and compared the Orphic Tradition with the works of Plato, Parmenides, and Plotinus. Furthermore, Raphael has written several books on the pathway of non-duality (*Advaita*). He has also translated and commented on a number of key Vedantic texts from the original Sanskrit.

With reference to Platonism, Raphael has highlighted the fact that, if we were to draw a parallel between Śaṅkara's *Advaita Vedānta* and a Traditional Western Philosophical Vision, we could refer to the Vision presented by Plato. Drawing such a parallel does not imply a search for reciprocal influences, but rather it points to something of paramount importance: a sole Truth, inherent in the doctrines (teachings) of several great thinkers, who, although far apart in time and space, have reached similar and in some cases even identical conclusions.

One notices how Raphael's writings aim to manifest and underscore the Unity of Tradition from the metaphysical perspective. This does not mean that he is in opposition to a dualistic perspective, or to the various religious faiths or 'points of view'.

An embodied real metaphysical Vision cannot be opposed to anything. What counts for Raphael is the unveiling, through living and being, which one has been able to contemplate.

In the light of the Unity of Tradition Raphael's writings or commentaries offer the intuition of the reader precise points of correspondence between Eastern and Western Teachings. These points of reference are useful for those who want to approach a comparative doctrinal study and to enter the spirit of the Unity of the Teaching.

For those who follow either the Eastern or the Western traditional line these correspondences help in comprehending how the *Philosophia Perennis* (Universal Tradition), which has no history and has not been formulated by human minds as such, 'comprehends universal truths that do not belong to any people or any age'. It is only for lack of 'comprehension' or 'synthetic vision' that one particular Branch is considered the only reliable one. From this position there can be only opposition and fanaticism. What degrades the Teaching is sentimental, fanatical devotionalism as well as proud intellectualism, which is critical and sterile, dogmatic and separative.

In Raphael's words: 'For those of us who aim at Realisation, it is our task is to get to the essence of every Teaching, because we know that, just as Truth is one, so Tradition is one even if, just like Truth, Tradition may be viewed from a plurality of apparently different points of view. We must abandon all disquisitions concerning the phenomenal process of becoming, and move onto the plane of Being.

In other words, we must have a Philosophy of Being as the foundation of our search and of our realisation."[1]

Raphael interprets spiritual practice as a 'Pathway of Fire'. Here is what he writes: 'The "Path of Fire" is the pathway which each disciple follows in all branches of the Tradition; it is the Way of Return. Therefore, it is not the particular teaching of an individual or the path parallel to the one and only Main Road... After all, every disciple follows his own "Path of Fire", no matter which Branch of the Tradition he belongs to'.

In Raphael's view, what is important is to express through living and being the truth that one has been able to contemplate. Thus, for each being, one's expression of thought and action must be coherent and in agreement with one's own specific *dharma*.

After more than 60 years of teaching, in both oral and written format, Raphael withdrew into *mahāsamādhī*.

* * *

May Raphael's Consciousness, an expression of Unity of Tradition, guide and illumine along this *Opus* all those who donate their *mens informalis* (formless mind) to the attainment of the highest known Realisation.

---

[1] See Raphael, *Tat tvam asi*, (That thou art). Aurea Vidyā, New York

PUBLICATIONS

Aurea Vidyā Collection

1. Raphael, ***The Threefold Pathway of Fire***, Thoughts that Vibrate for an Alchemical, Æsthetical, and Metaphysical ascesis
Retail ISBN 978-1-931406-00-0
Amazon 978-1-931406-00-0
Apple etal. 978-1-931406-46-8 forthcoming

2. Raphael, ***At the Source of Life***, Questions and Answers concerning the Ultimate Reality
Retail ISBN 978-1-931406-01-7
Amazon 979-8-576124-75-6
Apple etal. 978-1-931406-32-1

3. Raphael, ***Beyond the illusion of the ego***, Synthesis of a Realizative Process
Retail ISBN 978-1-931406-03-1
Amazon 978-1-931406-03-1
Apple etal. 978-1-931406-18-5 forthcoming

4. Raphael, ***Tat tvam asi***, That thou art, The Path of Fire According to the Asparśavāda
Retail ISBN 978-1-931406-02-4
Amazon 979-8-583067-52-7
Apple etal. 978-1-931406-34-5

5. Gauḍapāda, ***Māṇḍūkyakārikā***, The Metaphysical Path of *Vedānta**
Retail ISBN 978-1-931406-04-8
Amazon 978-1-931406-04-8
Apple etal. 978-1-931406-45-1 forthcoming

6. Raphael, ***Orphism and the Initiatory Tradition***

Retail ISBN 979-8-539590-78-9
Amazon 978-1-931406-05-5
Apple etal. 978-1-931406-35-2

7. Śaṅkara, ***Ātmabodha***, Self-knowledge*

Retail ISBN 978-1-931406-06-2
Amazon 978-1-931406-06-2
Apple etal. 978-1-931406-53-6 forthcoming

8. Raphael, ***Initiation into the Philosophy of Plato***

Retail ISBN 978-1-931406-07-9
Amazon 978-1-466486-98-0
Apple etal. 978-1-931406-52-9

9. Śaṅkara, ***Vivekacūḍāmaṇi***, The Crest-jewel of Discernment*

Retail ISBN 978-1-931406-08-6
Amazon 978-1-931406-08-6
Apple etal. 978-1-931406-48-2 forthcoming

10. ***Dṛdṛśyaviveka***, A philosophical investigation into the nature of the 'Seer' and the 'seen'*

Retail ISBN 978-1-931406-09-3
Amazon 979-8-669178-69-7
Apple etal. 978-1-931406-28-4

11. Parmenides, ***On the Order of Nature***, Περί φύσεως, For a Philosophical Ascesis*

Retail ISBN 978-1-931406-10-9
Amazon 979-8-698821-95-3
Apple etal. 978-1-931406-22-2

12. Raphael, ***The Science of Love***, From the desire of the senses to the Intellect of Love

Retail ISBN 978-1-931406-12-3
Amazon 978-1-931406-12-3
Apple etal. 978-1-931406-54-3 forthcoming

13. Vyāsa, ***Bhagavadgītā***, The Celestial Song*
Retail ISBN 978-1-931406-13-0
Amazon 979-8-562809-02-5
Apple etal. 978-1-931406-50-5

14. Raphael, ***The Pathway of Fire according to the Qabbālāh*** (Ehjeh 'Ašer 'Ehjeh), I am That I am
Retail ISBN 978-1-931406-14-7
Amazon 978-1-931406-14-7
Apple etal. 978-1-931406-49-9 forthcoming

15. Patañjali, ***The Regal Way to Realization***, Yogadarśana*
Retail ISBN 978-1-931406-15-4
Amazon 978-1-931406-15-4
Apple etal. 978-1-931406-20-8

16. Raphael, ***Beyond Doubt***, Approaches to Non-duality
Retail ISBN 978-1-931406-16-1
Amazon 979-8-657281-16-3
Apple etal. 978-1-931406-25-3

17. Bādarāyaṇa, ***Brahmasūtra****
Retail ISBN 978-1-931406-17-8
Amazon 978-1-931406-17-8
Apple etal. 978-1-931406-47-5 forthcoming

18. Śaṅkara, ***Aparokṣānubhūti***, Self-realization*
Retail ISBN 978-1-931406-23-9
Amazon 978-1-931406-19-2
Apple etal. 978-1-931406-30-7

19. Raphael, ***The Pathway of Non-Duality***, Advaitavāda
Retail ISBN 978-1-931406-21-5
Amazon 979-8-552322-16-9
Apple etal. 978-1-931406-24-6

20. ***Five Upaniṣads***, Īśa, Kaivalya, Sarvasāra, Amṛtabindu, Atharvaśira*
Retail ISBN 978-1-931406-26-0
Amazon 978-1-931406-26-0
Apple etal. 978-1-931406-29-1

21. Raphael, ***The Philosophy of Being,*** A conception of life for coming out of the turmoil of individual and social conflict

Retail ISBN 978-1-931406-27-7
Amazon 979-8-630006-39-4
Apple etal. 978-1-931406-31-4

22. Raphael, ***Awakening***

Retail ISBN 978-1-931406-44-4
Amazon 979-8-716953-07-9
Apple etal. 978-1-931406-33-8

23. Raphael, ***Essence and Purpose of Yoga***, Initiatory ways to the Transcendent

Retail ISBN 978-1-931406-36-9
Amazon 978-1-931406-61-1
Apple etal. 978-1-931406-62-8

Related Publications

A brief biography, ***Śaṅkara***
Aurea Vidyā. New York.

Retail ISBN 978-1-931406-11-6
Amazon 978-1-931406-11-6

Forthcoming Publications

Māṇḍūkya Upaniṣad, with the Gauḍapāda's *kārikā*s and the Commentary of Śaṅkara*

Retail ISBN 978-1-931406-37-6
Amazon 978-1-931406-57-4
Apple etal. 978-1-931406-58-1

Śaṅkara, ***Short Works***, Treatises and Hymns*

Retail ISBN 978-1-931406-71-0
Amazon 978-1-931406-55-0
Apple etal. 978-1-931406-56-7

Upaniṣads*

Retail ISBN 978-1-931406-38-3
Amazon 978-1-931406-59-8
Apple etal. 978-1-931406-60-4

Self-knowledge, The Harmonization of Psychic Energy. Edited by the Kevala Group

Retail ISBN 978-1-931406-40-6
Amazon 978-1-931406-63-5
Apple etal. 978-1-931406-64-2

Uttaragītā*

Retail ISBN 978-1-931406-68-0
Amazon 978-1-931406-69-7
Apple etal. 978-1-931406-70-3

Sanskrit Glossary

Retail ISBN 978-1-931406-67-3
Amazon 978-1-931406-65-9
Apple etal. 978-1-931406-66-6

* Translation from Sanskrit or Greek and Commentary by Raphael.

Aurea Vidyā is the Publishing House of the Parmenides Traditional Philosophy Foundation, a Not-for-Profit Organization whose purpose is to make Perennial Philosophy accessible.

The Foundation goes about its purpose in a number of ways: by publishing and distributing Traditional Philosophy texts with Aurea Vidyā, by offering individual and group encounters, by providing a Reading Room and daily Meditations at its Center.

* * *

Those readers who have an interest in Traditional Philosophy are welcome to contact the Foundation at:
parmenides.foundation@earthlink.net.

www.ingramcontent.com/pod-product-compliance
Lightning Source LLC
Chambersburg PA
CBHW032002080426
42735CB00007B/481
* 9 7 8 1 9 3 1 4 0 6 3 6 9 *